The Epistle of the Holy Apostle Paul to Titus

A Plain and Clear Exposition.

Interpreter
Aegidius Hunnius,
Doctor of Sacred Theology,
& Professor at the University of Marburg.

Marburg,
Printed by Paul Egenolph, Academic Printer.

Repristination Press
Malone, Texas

First edition, January 2024.

REPRISTINATION PRESS
716 HCR 3424 E MALONE, TEXAS 76660

www.repristinationpress.com

ISBN (10): 1-891469-82-7
ISBN (13): 978-1-891469-82-4

Table of Contents

FOREWORD.

Repristination Press has published several of Aegidius Hunnius' works over the years and his annotations on Titus offer
further evidence for the importance of his writings for the Evangelical Lutheran Church. *Epistolae divi Pauli Apostoli ad Titum,*
...(1592) is a representative sample of his exegetical writings. As
was common for early Lutheran theologians, Hunnius' *Titus* is not
a "commentary" in the modern sense of the term; rather, the author
offers brief annotations on points in the text which he perceived to
be particularly noteworthy. Much of the text is given over to "Loci
Communes"—"Common Places"—a tradition extending back to
Philip Melanchthon's 1521 *Loci Communes* in which the first Lutheran dogmatics textbook grew out of Melanchthon's lectures on
St. Paul's Epistle to the Romans. Hunnius' primary effort is emphasizing the dogmatic content of the epistle, applying the text to
the life of the Church. The necessity of faithful teaching and godliness (*pietatis*) are intertwined throughout Hunnius' annotations
and "Common Places."

A few points should be made regarding the translated text.
Adapting the publication of this translation to modern publishing
practices, the original marginal notes have been interpolated into
the text, delineating such passages and references by surrounding
them with braces ({}). On many occasions we have included the
original Latin and Greek words of Hunnius' text, or added words
for the sake of clarity, marking such occurrences with brackets ([]).
Additionally, the reader should understand that the original text
was published in an italic font with the original publisher using
the Roman font to emphasize words or passages which Hunnius
quoted from the biblical text. Since such a use of italics would be

distracting to the modern reader, we have rendered the main body of the text in the customary Roman font, using bold to distinguish those words and passages which Hunnius emphasized. (This substitution was commonly used in nineteenth century editions of Reformation/Post-Reformation texts.) Furthermore, on most occasions we have followed the author's lead with regard to emphasizing certain words by capitalizing the entire word. While such a usage is not customary in modern scholarship, it was a common practice in the sixteenth century.

It is the established practice of Repristination Press not to bury the text in footnotes; a few notes have been added for clarity, or to briefly delineate historical figures referenced by the author. We choose to let the author speak for himself.

One translation decision is worth noting. The word φιλανθρωπία has generally been translated as "philanthropy" throughout this book since this carries the sense in which Hunnius uses it. As the author observed, "As the Latin language cannot render [φιλανθρωπία] in one word, so the force of its emphasis cannot be matched by any power of human eloquence." (p. 120) Therefore, we have retained Hunnius' usage; readers certainly may consult standard Greek reference works if they desire to pursue the matter further.

Rt. Rev. James D. Heiser

The Festival of St. Titus, Bishop and Confessor, A.D. 2024

To the Reverend and Distinguished Men, Masters Johann and Ludwig Stippius, brothers: and also Master Johann Dipelius, the Most Faithful Ministers of the Church of God in Upper Hesse: likewise to Master Caspar Dipelius, the Most Diligent Headmaster of the School at Frankenberg, Lords, Friends, and Brothers in Christ,

Greetings, Grace, and Peace from God the Father, and the Lord Jesus Christ.

When the blessed Apostle Paul wanted to explain the reasons for his role and what and how much should be thought of him in the preaching of the doctrine of the Gospel, he writes in this manner to his Corinthians: "We function in the name of Christ's embassy, as if God implores you through us: we plead on behalf of Christ, be reconciled to God."

This sentiment is most worthy to be always kept in mind by all Christians—especially those whom God has raised to the pinnacle of ecclesiastical duty—and to be always weighed with careful study and diligence, in order that, with a deeper understanding of the majesty of the office they exercise, they may know themselves as obligated in religious gratitude towards Him who has mercifully placed them in that sublime station, and thus remember to conduct themselves more sacredly in such a venerable and splendid Ministry. Since, therefore, the Epistle of the blessed Paul, which he addressed to Titus, the Bishop of the churches of Crete, is almost entirely occupied with this type of theme, instructing the Ministers of the Divine Word concerning the qualities with which they should be adorned, and the virtues that should mark those who are called to manage the governance of the churches, so that neither packsaddles be put on oxen, nor mysteries be thought fit to be carried by donkeys, nor the holy be given to dogs, nor pearls to swine: It will not be inappropriate to preface a few words from Paul's wisdom about the dignity of the Ecclesiastical Ministry, by demonstrating which, it will naturally become evident how sacredly and with integrity one must conduct oneself in its administration.

Therefore, in the first place, is not the august dignity and magnitude of the ecclesiastical office wonderfully distinguished from the rest of the offices of this world and immensely exalted, in that the blessed Apostle does not hesitate to profess of himself and his colleagues and companions in this illustrious function, that they perform an embassy for Christ? It is considered distinguished in human affairs to be an Envoy of a Prince, King, or Emperor. Such is also the breadth and dignity of this office that whether one receives an envoy honorably or treats him contemptuously, all of it reflects upon the Lord whose envoy he is. How much more rightfully, then, is the honor considered sublime, if one acts as an envoy in the most holy Ministry of the Divine Word—not of an earthly prince or monarch who will soon perish along with his glory, but of the Lord and Savior of the whole world, Jesus Christ, He who alone has immortality and is called the King of kings, and Lord of lords. He who wishes His messengers and envoys to the human race to be regarded as supremely sacred and inviolable by divine right, thus speaks to His Apostles, and in their person to all sincere Teachers of the Church, saying: "He who hears you, hears Me; he who despises you, despises Me." Hence those praises of the Ministers of the Word, that they are proclaimed as the 'Envoys of God,' and 'Angels of the Lord God of hosts'; also as Messengers, who, as if dispatched from the heavenly court, reveal to mankind the will of God, and bring forth into the light of men from the abyss of divine Majesty. As St. Paul writes with heartfelt gratitude: "To me, the least of all the saints, this grace was given, to preach among the Gentiles the unsearchable riches of Christ, and to make all see what is the fellowship of the mystery, which from the beginning of the ages has been hidden in God." And regarding the Teachers of the New Testament in general (though it primarily refers to the Apostles), Isaiah says, and Paul says following Isaiah: "How beautiful are the feet of those who preach the gospel of peace, who bring glad tidings of good things, and who say unto Zion, Your God reigns." By no means should we overlook what Paul adds: That God Himself, through the Apostles and their successors in the Ministry, begs and entreats men to allow themselves to be reconciled to God. This contributes greatly to the magnification of the majesty of the Ecclesiastical Ministry (since the Ministers are as the mouth of God, and themselves a living letter to the human race), and at the same time, it opens up and presents for deeper contemplation with the eye of faith that philanthropic [φιλάνθρωπον][1] heart of our Savior God. For what, by the immortal God, is sweeter to say or more delightful and endearing to hear, than that the sublime divine Majesty, through the Ministry which He has ordained among men, condescends to such familiarity, that through His servants and envoys He urges us to gracious reconciliation, and freely offers amnesty and the eternal abolition of all offenses with which we have provoked His infinite justice to wrath? Oh, the never sufficiently praised and celebrated goodness and mercy of our supreme benefactor, God. Which earthly prince was ever endowed with such condescension, that if he were gravely offended by a subject, he himself would spontaneously offer reconciliation through envoys and messengers sent for this

---

1 Hunnius' use of φιλάνθρωπος throughout this work is translated according to the cognate, "philanthropy," etc., because of the way in which the author uses the term. In Hunnius' words, "As the Latin language cannot render it in one word, so the force of its emphasis cannot be matched by any power of human eloquence."

purpose, and moreover, seek it with entreaties? This, then, is what that blessed and sole Prince, God, does daily towards us in the ministry of the Word, as Paul testifies with clear and eloquent voice. And what He declares through the Prophet—that He stretches out His hands all day to a people, even if they are rebellious and stubborn—He does the same every day through the regular ministry of His divine Word. For when the ministers teach in accordance with the canon of the Sacred Scripture, it is God Himself who teaches. When they beseech us in the name of God and Christ and turn their speech in almost every form suited for persuasion, admonishing, arguing, commanding, rebuking, entreating, let us remember that this arises not from human will, but uniquely from the paternal affection of God, who desires to save us. When, in this way, people are absolved from sins by the voice [of the ministers], those who are absolved should consider that this absolution originates from the servants and envoys of God, and they should receive it no differently than if the voice of God were sounding from heaven to each one of them individually, saying: "Take heart, My son, your sins are forgiven." For what the Teachers of the Churches do and say in this regard, they perform only according to prescription. This is clearly professed by the Apostle in his own person, daring not to speak anything except what Christ accomplishes in him. He said of the ministry of reconciliation, entrusted to the Apostles by a special grace: "Whose sins you forgive, they are forgiven unto them; and whatever you bind on earth, shall be bound in heaven." Just as, conversely, those lawful sermons concerning the wrath of God and the coming temporal and eternal punishments for the impenitent are not empty scares, nor ineffective warnings, but the thunder of the omnipotent God, heavy with the lightning of eternal damnation, according to the unequivocal assertion of Christ: "Whose sins you retain, they are retained."

All these things, briefly mentioned up to this point, indeed come to the attention of the listeners, so that a more devout obedience may be established in their hearts towards their ordinary Church Pastors. For the respect given to these ministers of the Gospel is offered to God, not to men; and conversely, it is God who is denied when they refuse to pay due respect to their Preachers. In such disobedience, it is not men who are scorned, but God, who has given and bestowed His Holy Spirit as the guide of the ministry, as Paul affirmed to the Thessalonians.

These things must be noted by the Pastors so that they may perform the work of the Lord not sluggishly or deceitfully, but actively and diligently; knowing that they should do nothing except as prescribed in this embassy, that they keep themselves within the limits of this mandate: "Teach them to observe all that I have commanded you"; and finally, considering the dignity of the office, they should see it as their duty not to disgrace it in any way through impiety in life or dissolution of morals, and thus expose it to the reproaches of the world and the insults of Satan, or provide an occasion for scandals. About these, they will render an account to the Judge of the living and the dead, all the more serious as the office they have dishonored with the turpitude of life and morals is holier and more excellent.

As all these things are separately and more fully delivered in the Explanation of this Epistle to Titus. It [i.e., this Epistle] should be almost proprietary to the ministers of the Church, and although it is brief, it is rightly to be learned thoroughly, so that they may carry it with them perpetually not just in sight, but in fresh memory, in heart and mind, as a standard and measure, by which they uniquely conform all parts of their office, indeed, even all actions of life. When they have done this, they will acquire for themselves a good standing and great freedom in the faith, which is in Christ Jesus, and when that Prince of Pastors [*Pastoru Princeps*] appears, they will receive the unfading crown of glory, which the Lord has promised to those who have labored diligently in His vineyard, fought the good fight, finished the course commendably, kept the faith and conscience, and shown themselves to be thoroughly proven.

To you, however, Reverend and Most Courteous Men, I have deemed these my studious works worthy of solemn dedication: because many of you have for many years now been providing service truly pleasing to God and beneficial and salutary to the Church itself as most commendable and holy sons of the Church's Ministry, and one among you so excels in the scholastic duty with his dexterity that he does not consider it sufficient to stop there, but diligently works in the rudiments of preaching to soon legitimately undertake that ecclesiastical office.

Furthermore, there is another reason why I cannot and should not forget the kindness you have shown me when, two years ago, our University was transferred to Frankenberg due to the plague raging in Marburg. To omit other things in silence: certainly, it is no small matter that you generously offered your own houses for us to live in without charge; that you liberally supplied me and mine with as much grain as was nearly sufficient for the entire time the University stayed in Frankenberg, and you did not allow yourselves to be persuaded to accept any payment for it; and altogether you embraced me with such humanity, as one could scarcely hope for from one's closest relatives. Since your love for me is based on a pleasant agreement in doctrine, it must be all the more certain and firm. Indeed, nothing so unites people as the unity of religious faith and a pious agreement in the profession of heavenly doctrine, just as the Book of Acts recounts of the disciples of the early Church, that the multitude of believers had one heart and one soul. Led by these reasons, I did not doubt that this dedication, as a symbol of our union in Christ, would be very welcome to you.

What remains, I commend each and all of you to the protection of God.

Yours sincerely,

Aegidius Hunnius, D.

Marburg, 29th August, the Year of the Incarnate Word 1587.

14

Occasion and Argument of the Epistle.

The most noble island of Crete, situated in the middle of the Sea (which, as Strabo writes, is washed by the Aegean and Cretan seas to the north, and by the Libyan sea to the south), was converted to the faith of Jesus Christ by St. Paul. Therefore, since it was very important that such a celebrated and large island (which is reported to encompass five hundred eighty-nine thousand paces in circumference) should persevere in the faith and obedience of the Gospel, the Apostle, looking out for it most rightly, appointed Titus, his disciple, a man excelling in the knowledge of Sacred Scriptures and in piety, as Bishop.

Although Titus was doing his duty willingly, the magnitude of the matter, which was a concern to the Apostle, and the hidden attempts of Satan, who through Judaizing pseudo-apostles was trying to disturb the still tender Cretan churches, compelled him to write this Epistle. In it, he admonishes Titus to appoint suitable Presbyters or Teachers in each of the cities (of which, according to the consensus of Historians, as well as Virgil's Book 3 of the *Aeneid*, there were a hundred), noting precisely what qualities they should be adorned with; he also warns diligently against admitting those vain talkers and pseudo-teachers, preoccupied with Jewish fables and the precepts of men, to the ministry, but to strongly repel them. Soon, he instructs Titus on how he should exhort people of every order, sex, condition, and age to holy duty, taking his argument especially from God's saving grace and philanthropy, which appeared in this, that men redeemed from iniquity should show themselves to be followers of good works. He also instructs to avoid useless questions and the authors of sects, and if they do not come to their senses after being admonished, to be wary of them. Finally, entrusting some private and personal matters to Titus, he ends the entire Epistle with a pious salutation.

+++++

Argument of the First Chapter.

Paul, after the epigraph of the Epistle, admonishes Titus to complete the work begun and to establish Presbyters town by town in the island of Crete, at the same time teaching the qualities and characteristics such persons should be marked by.

He then encourages Titus to refute the pseudo-apostles and not to admit them to this most ample office.

Thus, there are three parts to this Chapter. The first, the epigraph with the salutation. The second, a reminder about the appointment of Presbyters town by town, and their qualities. The third, about repelling the pseudo-apostles.

+++++

FIRST PART.

Paul, a servant of God, etc.) Since in this Epistle, Divine Paul addresses future [battles] against the pseudo-apostles, who were trying to impose certain Judaic practices on the churches, he did not want to simply put his name in the subscription, but to add such titles of praise and commendation that would defend and vindicate his ministry from all human contempt. Therefore, at the beginning, due to his profession of faith, he calls himself "servant of God," that is, a true Christian, who has devoted himself entirely to God for holy services; but in terms of his office, [he calls himself an] "Apostle," that is, messenger or envoy of JESUS CHRIST, the

envoy of Him who is the King of kings, and Lord of lords. Furthermore, Paul explains the condition of his office by its circumstances,
and, at the same time, amplifies the dignity of the entrusted function. For he says that he is an Apostle of Christ, **according to the
faith of God's elect, and the acknowledgment of the truth**. Here
he designates the goal and faith of his embassy as this: To lead
men to the faith common to all the elect (by which alone they are
saved) and to the recognition of the saving truth: But of truth, not
that philosophical kind which brings delight for a short time, but
that **which is according to** religious **godliness**, whose fruit extends
and manifests itself into that truly blessed other life. For it is ac-
companied by **the hope of eternal life**. And this hope is not at all
uncertain, but completely infallible. He shows this from the nature
of the promising God, adding: **which God, who cannot lie, promised**. Paul extols this from the circumstance of antiquity, since he
says it was **promised before the world began**. Here, by the word
promise, he indicates that this hope of everlasting life was destined
for us in that very eternal council of God's Predestination, before
there were any temporal ages; and, as soon as these began, it was
also immediately promised in Paradise to the first humans; namely,
through the preaching about the seed of the woman, which would
crush the serpent's head.

　　But has in due times manifested, etc.) To the promise, by
which that which the Lord had destined for us from eternity and
had promised from the beginning of the world, Saint Paul contrasts the fulfillment of the matter itself, asserting that the hope
once promised has now been revealed in the fullness of time. Although this mystery was known to the Prophets and other faithful
under the Old Testament to the extent necessary for their salvation, it was still veiled in the shadows of figures and wrapped in
the clouds of various ceremonies, and Christ Himself had not yet
come, nor had the events promised by the Lord about the sending

of the Son occurred; much less were these things revealed to the Gentiles. Hence it appears that the revelation of this was not extended in only one way in the Kingdom of the Messiah. But now, with Christ presented, **God has manifested His word**, namely the Gospel of salvation, **through preaching**, by which He wished to make known to the human race, not in just one nation alone but in all nations and peoples whatsoever.

Which is committed to me, etc.) He declares that this task of bringing forth into the light the hope once promised has been sacredly delegated and entrusted to him. Indeed, it was not by the judgment or command of any man, but **by the command of JE-SUS CHRIST**, by whom he himself was called from heaven to this arduous duty and was instructed in the School of Paradise with sufficient knowledge for this task. He calls Christ by the august and comforting name of **Savior** God, for He is the sole Savior of the human race, outside of whom there is no salvation nor any other Savior. He is also **God**, thereby possessing the powerful ability to save, and who could also authoritatively delegate this mission of preaching to the Apostle.

Thus far, indeed, is the first part of the Epigraph, namely the subscription, which identifies the name of the Author of the Epistle. Now follows the second part, which declares the name of the person to whom this is written.

To Titus, my true son, etc.) Who this Titus was is well known from the Pauline Epistles, in which his name is frequently mentioned—born, evidently, to Greek or Gentile parents. The Holy Apostle Paul took him several times as a companion and colleague on his journeys, as in Galatians 2, and he refused to circumcise him to assert the freedom of the Gospel against the pseudo-apostles. Paul calls him his companion in 2 Corinthians 8, and judges him suitable and trustworthy for collecting the alms from the Gentile churches for the use of the poor in Judea who were struggling with famine. He also deemed him worthy to be appointed as Bishop over the most ample and noble island of Crete. Therefore, due to his proven faith and piety, he does not hesitate to call him his **true son**. Indeed, a son, since Paul himself had begotten him in Christ Jesus through the Gospel, had won him for Christ, and embraced him as a father embraces a son with genuine affection of charity. For the sake of explanation, he adds, **according to the common faith**, to teach in what sense he calls him his son; namely, because he had brought him to the communion of faith through his ministry. He calls him not simply a son, but a γνήσιον or **true** son: because he was not a hypocrite, but with his fervent zeal and dedication to advancing the doctrine of the Gospel, he represented the incredible affection of the Apostle, who considered the glory of Christ, the course of the Church, and the salvation of all men more precious than all the goods and treasures of this world. This affection was not obscurely shining in Titus himself, and therefore he showed himself to be a γνήσιον τέκνον, a true son, of such a great Apostle.

Grace, mercy, etc.) The salutation is plainly Evangelical, customary for Paul in all his Epistles, in which he prays for **grace** from God for his Titus, meaning His gratuitous and paternal favor and love, and whatever freely comes from this love to men. He also prays for that **mercy** of God, by which He kindly accepts men, although naturally miserable sinners and deserving of damnation, into grace, with sins forgiven for the sake of Christ. Thirdly, he wishes **peace**, which, as is the custom of the Hebrews, includes all sought-after gifts and benefits, both spiritual and physical. The Holy Apostle understands this peace of conscience to arise from a vivid sense of the grace and mercy of a reconciled God. And all these things indeed he wishes for Titus, from Him who alone can and is accustomed to give them, namely **from God the Father**, as the primary source of all overflowing goodness towards us, and

from Jesus Christ, through whom, as through a Channel, all of this grace, mercy, and peace of conscience is derived to us. He calls Him **Lord**, both by reason of *Nature*, because He is true God, and by reason of *Office*, because He has purchased us with His own blood. Hence, he also calls Him **Savior**, who saved us when we were lost and powerfully rescued us from the jaws of hell.

Common Places. [Loci Communes.]

First. Let us recall the words of Paul, soon after his conversion to a servant of God and an Apostle of Jesus Christ: The immense goodness of God should come to our minds, which alone accomplished it that an enemy of the Gospel—so fierce, so cruel, so sworn to the destruction of the Church—would come to his senses from the snares of the devil and, having been converted to the faith of Jesus Christ, would now propagate with incredible zeal and effort the doctrine he once intensely hated and persecuted. Just as he himself presents this joyful and amazing conversion as a mirror of the patience and mercy of God in 1 Timothy 1.

Second. When Paul calls himself a servant of God, he wants all Christians to be reminded of their duty by this title. For we, too, are servants of God, both by our general profession of piety and in our specific calling [*vocatione*]. Having been freed from sin, we have become servants of God and of righteousness. [Romans 6] Not that we serve Him with a spirit of servility, as in Romans 8. For by this name Christ no longer calls us servants, but friends [John 15], indeed brothers and co-heirs (John 20, Romans 8). But because we have been redeemed by Him, we are no longer our own, but are committed to His holy service. Therefore, let us strive to be among those faithful servants whose fidelity is proclaimed in the parable in Luke 12. And, as the Apostle advises, in our general calling, let us present our members as servants of righteousness for sanctification (Romans 6). And in our specific calling, let each be faithful and diligently labor according to the talent entrusted to them (Matthew 25).

Third. Concerning the dignity of the ecclesiastical ministry, of which the very word "Apostle" reminds us. Although the august name of the Apostles primarily belongs to those extraordinary servants of Christ, commonly called Apostles, κατ᾽ ἐξοχήν [by way of eminence], because of their universal mission and dispatch, not to any particular place or to any specific people, but to the whole world, to preach the Gospel to every creature (hence their calling was not tied to any particular place), secondarily, this very appellation suits and is appropriate for the doctors and ministers of any churches, who all likewise function in an embassy for Christ, imploring in Christ's stead, men, to allow themselves to be reconciled with God (2 Corinthians 5). Therefore, the preaching of those ministers, who are legitimately called and proclaim the pure Word of God, should be received as the speech of God's envoys by the listeners [1 Thessalonians 2], from whom the Lord does not want them to be despised any more than any earthly monarch can bear the contempt of his envoys, according to this: "He who hears you, hears Me; he who despises you, despises Me" (Luke 10).

Fourth. The same should also motivate the ministers not to carry out their divine office negligently, reluctantly, or for shameful gain, but with a willing mind and voluntarily, as in 1 Peter 5. And indeed with tireless effort, in season and out of season, as in 2 Timothy 4, presenting the pure and uncorrupted Word of God, and adorning their ministry with chastity of life, so that they may be examples to the flock (1 Peter 5), and models of the faithful in speech, in conduct, in love, in spirit, in faith, in purity [1 Timothy 4]. Such will acquire for themselves a good standing and great boldness in the faith which is in Christ Jesus, and will eventually receive an unfading crown of glory (1 Peter 5, Daniel 12, 2 Timothy 4); as is promised to the Teachers of the Churches of Smyrna and Philadelphia in Revelation 2 and 3.

Fifth. From the words, "according to the common faith of the elect," we learn that the elect are not to be sought outside the assembly of believers. For those who do not believe are not saved; just as God has never decreed or chosen to save those who were not going to believe, but rather those who were going to follow the order established by God for the attainment of faith, and through that order and means, were going to come to faith and persevere in it. According to the saying: "As many as were ordained to eternal life believed" [Acts 13].

Sixth. The Apostle also teaches that there is one faith for all the elect, by which they are saved; hence, shortly thereafter he calls it the common faith. Therefore, it is futile what the Scholastics have devised, imagining various different ways to heaven, saying that the Fathers before the Law were saved by the Law of Nature, the Jews by the Law of Moses, and Christians by the Law of the Gospel. It is also a fiction of the devil, which keeps many people in errors, while claiming that everyone can be blessed in their own Religion, as long as they otherwise live civilly well and honorably. But Scripture shows us only one saving faith, which rests in the trust in Christ, only one way to the Father, which is Christ Himself (John 14), through whom the Fathers of old were saved, just as we are; and we, just as they (Acts 15). Those who are ignorant of this way will hear: "I do not know you."

Seventh. This same common faith of the elect (as Paul has chosen to name it) teaches us about the close bond that unites Christians. Indeed, there is nothing that so binds the hearts of people together as the unity of faith, as we read in Acts: "The multitude of those who believed were of one heart and one soul." [Acts 4] This is also the reason why the Apostle, taking his argument from the unity of faith, exhorts to nurture a consensus of minds and mutual charity (Ephesians 4).

Eighth. The recognition of the truth, which Paul mentions here, should be esteemed. Philosophers have thought that life should rightly be spent in the pursuit of truth. They placed the entire sum of their happiness in it. They promoted the contemplation of truth as the highest good. And indeed, it cannot be denied that the knowledge of truth even in matters of philosophy and subjects of human reason has its own use, pleasure, and delight. However, if we weigh the matter in a just balance, it is certain that the knowledge of theological wisdom and truth is truly the highest good, since it alone contemplates God—who is otherwise unknown to human philosophy—through the understanding of faith, and has as its object the highest good, GOD Himself, and Jesus Christ whom He sent: the usefulness of whose knowledge is not confined within the bounds of this age, but extends into the next life (John 17).

Ninth. And because that knowledge of truth, which the Apostle writes he is called to teach, is "according to godliness," let the Pastors of the churches learn to avoid old wives' fables and useless, thorny, and idle questions, which do nothing for the edification of the listeners. Let this be their sole focus and goal in teaching: That they instruct and build up their listeners in godliness and impart useful things, just as the goal of all Scripture is the perpetual benefit of mankind (2 Timothy 3). And God Himself is an example for Preachers in this regard, who says through the Prophet in Isaiah 48, "I am the Lord your God, teaching you what is best." And Paul exhorts his Timothy to reject profane and old wives' fables, and instead to train himself in godliness. [1 Timothy 4]

Tenth. From the words: "In hope of eternal life, etc.," we are reminded of what the hope of Christians is; namely, the expectation of eternal life. Therefore, it has as its object not things that come into view. For if hope is seen, it is not hope, Paul says in Romans 8. But it [hope] has as its object things invisible in this life, and indeed (in terms of our perspective) future. This is where the difference between faith and hope lies: While both revolve around things not apparent, faith concerns not future things, but present ones, although not exposed to the eyes; namely, the grace of God, the forgiveness of sins, and the imputed righteousness of Christ, which are actually possessed in this age through faith. Indeed, faith can also be occupied with the past, as we understand by faith that the ages were once formed (Hebrews 11). Hope, however, revolves around things not only invisible, but also those that are awaited in the future. And because it has as its foundation not an opinion conceived from human thoughts, but the promises of the Word of God, hence it so happens that the hope of Christians cannot be deceived (Romans 5).

Eleventh. On the Nature of God, who is and remains eternally and unchangeably the truth, incapable of lying, as noted by the Apostle Paul. Therefore, it is piously considered among those things that God cannot do, just as He cannot be unjust, cannot sin, cannot die in His divine nature. These [impossibilities] are not attributed to any weakness of impotence, but, rather, to the praise of omnipotence. For if He could lie, be unjust, sin, or die in His Nature, He would not be God, and therefore He would not be omnipotent. And to this belong all things that we know from the Sacred Scriptures to be opposed to the Nature of God and which would destroy it. Apart from these, which Scripture itself testifies to be opposed to God's Nature, we are not allowed to imagine other things at the discretion of human reason that are impossible [ἀδύνατα] for God. Indeed, Scripture declares with a clear and resounding voice that nothing is impossible for God (Jeremiah 32, Zechariah 8, Luke 1), and even more so that He can do abundantly above all that we think (Ephesians 3). Therefore, they are rash who, without any testimony of the divine Word, either write or certainly determine in their heart, that it is impossible for God to make the very body of His Son, without the destruction of Essence, present in all those places where the Sacrament of the Eucharist is celebrated on earth. For since this presence rests on the institution of the Savior, and they cannot show its impossibility by any testimony of the Sacred Scriptures, it is clear that their opinion is built on sand and is ruinous. Nor do they escape when they rush to their 'refuge of contradictions' [χρησφύγετον], arguing that God does not want contradictions, since He is the eternal truth and cannot lie: "But these are contradictory, if it is said that Christ's body is in heaven, and yet also in the Eucharist celebrated on this earth." But we respond: "Not everything that reason thinks is contradictory should be immediately considered as such, but only those things which faith, based on the Word of God, shows to be contradictory [ἀντιφατικὰ]." Let us illustrate the matter with examples. To reason, "Nothing" and "Something" are contradictory. Yet Theology believes that not only something, but everything, has been produced from nothing, without any concern for the rules of contradiction. And thus by faith (not by reason) we understand that the ages were formed (Hebrews 11). Similarly, a man's body is devoured by beasts, and his flesh is turned into their flesh and blood, and yet the flesh and blood of the beasts will not rise again; but the flesh of the torn man, which had been converted into the flesh of the beast, will rise again. Which philosophy will reconcile these? Will not all philosophers cry out that it cannot be affirmed without manifest contradiction, that the flesh of that man should rise again, so that the beast's flesh does not rise, when indeed his flesh has truly been converted into that of the beast? Likewise, if Abraham had wanted to decide from his own mind about the contradictions and from there to deny the Word of God, how plausibly he could have done so? For who would not have seen these as contradictory: That kings and peoples would proceed from Isaac, and yet he was to be sacrificed before a single offspring was born from him? How ingeniously could reason have argued that contradictions cannot be simultaneously true, therefore this commandment to offer the son did not come from God, but from an evil spirit? But Abraham, setting aside all thoughts about contradictions, obeys the command of God, and reconciles by faith [Hebrews 11] what no reason could reconcile. However, if (as has been said) faith itself finds from the revealed Word that something is truly contradictory, and now not opposed to *reason* but to *faith*, there it rightly concludes that it cannot be true because God does not want contradictions, which according to the declaration of the revealed Word are such, because He cannot lie.

Twelfth. Concerning God's Providence in caring for human salvation, that before secular times [*tempora secularia*], He had such a precise plan for our salvation that He designated and promised by designating eternal life to all who would believe in the Son, the Savior of the world. In this sense, Christ says that the Kingdom of blessedness was prepared for the elect from the beginning of the world (Matthew 25). And the Apostle in Ephesians 1 testifies that we were chosen in Christ Jesus before the foundations of the world were laid; and writes that the grace, which has been made manifest through the appearance of our Savior Jesus Christ, was given to us through Jesus Christ before eternal times [*tempora aeterna*]. Hence shines forth God's burning love for us and His truly paternal care for our salvation.

Thirteenth. But from this we also learn that all human merit is excluded from the reason for our salvation. For eternal life was given and promised to us through that eternal election in Christ, and with respect to us entirely gratuitous, before eternal times, and thus before we had done anything either good or bad: so that it would be clear, God, in His merciful predestination, preceded all our effort or course by infinite ages, and in choosing us did not regard any good works, but only His Son, and His merit to be apprehended by faith.

Fourteenth. And because he mentions that hope of eternal life, promised before secular times, now made manifest through the preaching of the Gospel, he clearly confirms that the decree of our predestination, except for the unique things reserved to God (which, however, do not conflict with the will revealed in the Gospel), is no longer hidden but has now been revealed, so that, speaking most properly, the word of the Gospel is nothing other than the solemn revelation and announcement of that eternal decree regarding our salvation, which God had set forth within Himself, as the Apostle speaks. As this is repeatedly stated by Paul, especially in Ephesians 1, where, speaking expressly of predestination, he writes that God has made known to us the MYSTERY of His will, which He purposed in Himself, etc. Thus in Romans 16, he defines the Gospel as the proclamation or announcement and revelation of the mystery kept silent through eternal times, and now revealed according to the command of the eternal GOD to all nations. Therefore, whoever wants to know if he is elected, does not need to "walk in the air," nor to ascend to heaven with his thoughts, nor descend into the abyss; rather the word itself is near you, in your mouth and in your heart, clearly revealing and manifesting God's will to you (John 3 and 6, Romans 10).

Fifteenth. Since he asserts that the doctrine of the Gospel was revealed in these last times, so that although some promises were made in the Old Testament, now, through the appearance of Christ, the entire mystery of our salvation has been unfolded from the wrappings of ceremonies and brought into the clearest light of truth. From this, we are reminded of our happiness, for now our salvation is nearer than when we first believed; the night is far gone, the day is at hand (Romans 13). Hence Christ declares the ears and eyes of His disciples blessed, because they hear and see things which in former times kings and prophets desired to see and hear, but did not have the opportunity (Luke 10).

Sixteenth. When Paul writes that the preaching of the Gospel was committed to him according to the command of God our Savior, let preachers learn from this to be certain of their calling to the ministry, and to rejoice in the testimony of a good conscience, knowing that they have not seized or invaded such a great office by force, bribery, purchase, or other illegitimate means, nor have they run without being called, as in Jeremiah 23. But that according to the command of God our Savior, through ordinary and divine calling, this function has been entrusted to them. For even that calling, which is by the voice of the Church, we hear in the second part of this chapter, is ordinary and divine.

Seventeenth. The epithet that Paul attributes to God, calling Him the Savior, instructs us about His philanthropy [φιλανθρωπία]: that He desires to save the miserable human race, although it has fallen through disobedience, and does not wish anyone to perish (2 Peter 3). Hence, St. Paul, with words of utmost memorability and observance, calls Him the Savior of ALL MEN, especially of believers (1 Timothy 4). Indeed, of all men, insofar as He desires all men to be saved and to come to the knowledge of the truth (1 Timothy 2). But he says, especially of the faithful: "for they hear the word and attain faith from it." As for the others, they perish due to their own fault, not because of God, who, with respect to His will, bears this title, that He is the Savior of ALL Men, and does not even wish the death of the DYING (Ezekiel 33).

Eighteenth. The fact that Paul still considers it necessary to write in this way to Titus, who is already running well and performing his duty admirably, teaches us that no effort in pious and holy exhortations is superfluous. Even pious men and those regenerated by the Spirit of God, due to the inherent flaw of nature, innate depravity, and sluggishness, occasionally need spurs. Therefore, it is the duty of Church ministers to never slacken in their task, but to be insistent in season and out of season, to strengthen and encourage even those who are doing their duty, to awaken the hesitant and sleeping, to admonish the unruly, to comfort the faint-hearted (1 Thessalonians 5), to rebuke sinners, to fulfill all parts of their office, and to prove themselves fully. For the devil does not sleep or cease, but takes advantage of the drowsiness and negligence of teachers to spread his tares (Matthew 13). Therefore, let the ministers keep constant vigil, as if appointed watchmen (Ezekiel 33, Acts 20).

Nineteenth. We learn how we can truly be sons of the Prophets and Apostles from the example of Titus, whom Paul calls his own true son—certainly not in the way the Pope calls any Christians his sons (as if he were the universal Father of the Church, from whom the utmost of faith and salvation is to be expected). This fatherhood is owed solely to God (Matthew 23). But we are made sons of the Prophets and Apostles when, regenerated through their word, we follow them and emulate them, succeeding in their doctrine, imitating their faith, and zealously emulating their life and works. Just as those are the sons of Abraham who follow in the footsteps of his faith and perform his works (John 8 and Romans 4).

Twentieth. Regarding the salutation, which, if accepted in faith, holds the power of a blessing. The Savior speaks about the salutation of His disciples in Matthew 10. If they pray for peace upon a house or city, that peace will come upon it, provided that the house or city accepts and receives that salutation in faith. Hence, there is a devout custom for preachers to begin their sermons using almost the same formula, saying: "Grace, mercy, and peace from God the Father, and the Lord Jesus Christ." And when descending from the pulpit, they repeat either the same words or another of Paul's blessings: "The grace of our Lord Jesus Christ be with all of you." Or: "The grace of the Lord Jesus Christ, and the love of God, and the communion of the Holy Spirit be with all of you" [2 Corinthians 13]; and finally, they dismiss the congregation with that solemn blessing with which the Priests of the Old Testament were instructed to dismiss their congregation: "The Lord bless you and keep you: The Lord make His face shine upon you, and be gracious to you: The Lord lift up His countenance upon you, and give you peace" (Numbers 6).

Twenty-first. The same salutation teaches us what are the most excellent gifts and blessings of God that we should rightly pray for and desire for ourselves and others from God, namely the grace and mercy of God, bringing with them an infinite abundance not only of earthly goods, but much more of heavenly and eternal ones. This grace of God, and His favor, also makes the human heart peaceful. Indeed, this is the primary source and origin of our election, justification, and salvation. Therefore, let us strive to have a merciful and propitious God. For if He is for us, who can be against us? (Isaiah 51, Romans 8).

Twenty-second. This same salutation also teaches us who is the Author and Giver of these gifts—namely, grace, mercy, and peace— and from whom they should be sought and expected; namely, from God the Father and our Lord Jesus Christ. For every good and perfect gift (among which are chiefly the Grace of God and peace of conscience) comes down from the Father of lights (James 1).

Therefore, it is God who dignifies us with His gratuitous favor, who makes us dear through His beloved Son, Jesus Christ [Ephesians 1]. And it is Jesus Christ who has purchased and merited this grace of the Father with His blood; who, as the Prince of Peace [Isaiah 9], has restored lost peace, reconciling us to God through His blood [Colossians 1]; who, having poured out the Holy Spirit into our hearts, has made us peaceful; and thus bestows HIS peace upon us, not the temporal peace of the world (John 16), but spiritual and eternal, which surpasses all understanding (Philippians 4), in which the Kingdom of God consists (Romans 14), and upon which the pivot of our entire blessedness turns.

SECOND PART.

Now St. Paul approaches his principal undertaking. He advises Titus to remember that he was appointed to the island of Crete to complete the Reformation among the Cretans, begun through the Apostle's ministry. He should not only spread the word of the Gospel himself, but also appoint others suitable for teaching, and formally entrust and appoint them to the churches in each city.

Thus, the sense of the Apostle's words is: "After the Gospel was also received among the Cretans and churches were established there through my ministry, and since my duty, to which I am also obligated to other nations, did not allow me to remain on the island: 'I left you' in my place. And indeed, for two principal reasons. First, so that you might bring to completion and conclude the Reformation that I began. Secondly, so that you 'appoint Presbyters in every town.'" By 'Presbyters' he means the teachers or ministers of the churches, as this term is used in Acts 15 and 20, 1 Timothy 5, 1 Peter 5. However, Paul does not want Titus to admit just anyone to the office of the Presbyterate, but wants a careful selection to be made, according to the form he had previously prescribed to him: "as I directed you," he says. How, then, were they to be selected according to the Apostle's instructions? "If anyone is blameless, etc." Paul does not require that someone be free from all sin. For it seemed good to God to appoint in the ministry of the Gospel as teachers, not angels, but men, who themselves are encompassed with weaknesses. Therefore, He wants them to be "blameless" not with respect to God, in whose sight no one is either innocent or blameless (for even the heavens are not pure in His sight, and in His messengers, He finds fault, Job 4 and 15), but in terms of men. Here the word (ἀνέγκλητος/"blameless") is opposed both to perverse opinions in doctrine and to vices and crimes in life, with which He does not want the conduct of the Presbyters to be infamous. And indeed, this is a more general criterion extending to the whole course of the ministry.

A husband of one wife, etc.) This is the second criterion to be observed in selecting Presbyters or Pastors; namely, that one should be the husband of only one wife. But here someone might object: Are those who are unmarried, either due to youth or because they are endowed with the special gift of continence, not admitted to the ministry? I respond: The Apostle does not prohibit these from access to this office, provided they are otherwise suitable for managing the affairs of the Church and live chastely. But this criterion is set against those who avoid marriage because of its difficulties, even though they lack the gift of continence; similarly, against those who are bigamous or polygamous. The former, he wishes to have their own wives if they are to be tolerated in the ministry. The latter, those who had married more than one wife, he simply considers to be excluded from the ministry. And this admonition concerning the marital union with only one wife was at that time especially to be observed in the selection of ministers.

For since in the New Testament polygamy had been abolished and antiquated by the sentence of the Savior, and yet it frequently happened that those who had previously in paganism or Judaism taken several wives converted to the faith of Christ, whom they could not divorce for many reasons upon conversion (for the custom of divorcing was no less abolished), therefore such persons were indeed admitted to Christianity, but were not admitted to undertake the duties of the ministry, because polygamy, abolished by the word of Christ, would not be without scandals in such a holy office. From this, it is clear that it is futile to seek protection for polygamy in these words of the Apostle, as if it were thereby permitted to those outside the ministry of the Word. Otherwise, this specific prohibition of polygamy for ministers of the Word would not have seemed necessary, if the practice of polygamy had already been universally prohibited among all Christians. But there is no need to twist the words of the Holy Spirit, as the true reason has already been shown to be quite different, why in the early days of the emerging Gospel, it was necessary to warn against admitting polygamists to the Church's Presbytery. Nor does the Apostle's criterion oppose those who marry another after the death of their first spouse. For through the death of the first spouse, that marriage is completely dissolved, as Paul clearly teaches in Romans 7 and 1 Corinthians 7. Nor do such persons thereby become polygamous: for at one and the same time, they do not have several, but only one spouse in marriage.

Having faithful children) Just as he permits a Presbyter or Pastor of the Church to have a wife, so he also grants legitimate use of this union in the procreation of children. However, he should raise those whom he begets liberally in faith and piety: **that he may have faithful children.** Children are not born faithful from faithful parents, but are born naturally as children of wrath, like the others, Ephesians 2. The reason is that holy men generate according to the *flesh*, not the *spirit*. Hence it is said: "That which is born of the flesh is flesh." However, the Presbyter is advised to ensure that his children, given faith through Baptism, remain faithful and do not follow fanatical opinions, but sincerely uphold true and uncorrupted religion. In this matter, the diligent upbringing and liberal and careful education by the parents are of great importance, a salutary means through which the Lord preserves children in true religion, faith, and piety. Thus, Paul not only teaches how Bishops themselves should be chosen, but also what their children should be like, so that a conjecture can be made about the ministers' skill in governing the Church if they have indeed given a specimen of their industry in managing their own family.

Not open to the charge of debauchery, etc.) Just as he taught in a single word what the children of ministers of the Word should be like—namely, faithful, encompassing their purity in religion and integrity of morals arising from true faith—so now from the opposite perspective he teaches what they should not be; that is, what they should avoid. For he says: **Not open to the charge of debauchery**. The Greek text has: μη εν κατηγορια ασωτιας, as if Paul is saying: "The children of the teachers of the Word should not indulge in luxury or pursue indecent pleasures." From this, it follows that they could be publicly and privately accused by people, and there could be talk about their dissolute life in barber shops and baths, some stain might be cast upon their parents, and the ministry itself might be significantly disfigured.

Or who are not intractable) This second point is that which Paul wants to be alien to a Pastor's children. He understands, however, that stubborn defiance, by which they neither obey their own parents nor comply with others to whom they owe obedience, but grumble and resist their parents at home, and outside, they are reluctant to conform to magistrates, teachers, and elders.

For a bishop must be... etc.) The term **Bishop** in the highest degree [κατ᾽ ἐξοχην] indeed signifies those chief Pastors of the churches, to whom the oversight of the life and manners of other ministers is entrusted, whom we rightly call Superintendents today, from the force of this Greek appellation. However, when used by Paul, it often denotes any Pastor of the Church of God. For all other preachers of the Word are also overseers, and, in their own way, Superintendents and Bishops, ordained for this purpose, that, as if placed on watch, they should be vigilant and earnestly attentive, lest anything detrimental from the devil or his agents be brought to the churches over which they [the Pastors] are appointed. Just as Paul says the Presbyters, whom he had called from Ephesus to Miletus, were appointed by the Holy Spirit as Bishops, to shepherd the Church of God, which He purchased with His own blood. This general meaning is also taken in 1 Timothy 3. Therefore, the Apostle gives reason why he also wants the families of Bishops to be commended for integrity of life, because it is fitting and the dignity of the position demands that Bishops should be blameless in every aspect, so that no scandal arises from their own household, which should rightly be a school and workshop of piety and all virtues.

As a steward of God, etc.) This is a confirmation of reason, also drawn from the sources of what is honorable, in this sense: Every Bishop, by virtue of his office, is an *Oikonomos* or "steward of God," who in His house or Church, should handle the mysteries of God with as much fidelity and reverence as possible, and dispense them properly for edification, not destruction. Therefore, since the management of the Church is entrusted to him, he should strive to be a good steward in his own private house as well: He should ensure that nothing against duty is committed by his family, wife, and children, but he should restrain them within the bounds of what is right and honorable, as far as possible, through his authority, example, teachings, and admonitions.

Not stubborn, etc.) In prescribing the form of a true and praiseworthy Bishop, Paul in the following text maintains this order: first showing which vices to avoid, then which virtues those who are entrusted with the teaching office should pursue. Let us briefly go through both with a brief paraphrase, intending to discuss them more thoroughly in the explanation of doctrines.

Not stubborn) In Greek, it is αὐθάδης. An αὐθάδης is someone who is greatly pleased with his own words and deeds, admires himself, praises only himself, and looks down on everything of others from a lofty position. This vice, as inherently disgraceful, and also when associated with scandal in the Church, and very dangerous in a Bishop, is commanded to be absent from church ministers. For, if those who suffer from it once stray from the path of the Word, they find it exceedingly difficult to accept admonition and to be called back to the right way. Being swollen and inflated with the evil of αὐθαδεία [arrogance], they vehemently defend and protect their own views at great cost, so as not to appear to have erred.

Not quick-tempered) The blessed Apostle does not forbid just and fervent zeal for the glory of GOD, provided that it is sober and so tempered that it does not exceed the bounds, or be carried headlong beyond the set limits of right. Thus, he also does not simply disapprove of anger, which can often be praiseworthy. For when something is permitted that conflicts with the Word of God, with piety, and good morals, then indeed it is commendable to be angry, and shameful not to be. Hence, there is a difference between ὀργὴ or anger, which is the act of becoming angry and often exists even in those who do not suffer from the malady of wrath, and ὀργιλότης or quick-temperedness, which is not the act of becoming angry, but a perverted affect of nature, and an immoderate inclination to anger, for almost any trivial cause. It is this disposition that he wants to be as far as possible from the Pastors of the churches. For those who loosen the reins of their anger do everything tumultuously, and in the heat of the soul, often say or do things that destroy more than they build.

Not given to wine) This is the third item in the catalog of vices that the Apostle removes from the character of a suitable Bishop; namely, drunkenness. Here, he does not distinguish between *disposition* and *action*, so as to condemn either one merely by simple disapproval (as previously there could have been a distinction between anger and quick-temperedness, where anger could sometimes be praiseworthy). Paul condemns both drunkenness and the condition of being a drunkard equally.

Not violent) The fourth vice that is prohibited for a Bishop is not to be a striker, one who seeks to avenge perceived wrongs against himself with hands and arms.

Not greedy for dishonest gain) The fifth is αἰσχροκέρδεια (shameful greed), when a Minister, afflicted by the vice of avarice, engages in schemes for acquiring money, which are contrary to the office and dignity of the Holy Ministry; or in legitimate transactions allowed for a minister of the Word, he focuses on his own private gain and profit with the risk of causing offense and harm to others.

And indeed, these are vices that disqualify someone from being a good Bishop. Next follow the virtues and qualities required in Ministers, some of which commend their life and external conduct, while others pertain to, and affect, the duty of teaching.

First, that he be φιλόξενος, **hospitable**. Indeed, the Apostle wants the Bishop to be generous in receiving, helping, and reviving strangers, especially those of the household of faith, and those driven into exile for the sake of religion. Secondly, Paul requires in the bishopric or ministry a man who is φιλάγαθος, **a lover of good**, one who loves and pursues what is good and right, and is inclined to do good for anyone.

Third, he wants the same person to be **sober**, or, as the Greek word puts it, σώφρονα, meaning prudent and moderate, acting wisely and moderately in his actions.

He also wants him to be **just**, who in his external conduct, or in the permissible transactions of a Minister, does no injustice to anyone, nor indulges in personal biases, nor commits προσωποληψία (favoritism) in matters related to his ministry with his listeners, which is antagonistic to all justice and fairness.

He also describes him as **pious** or **holy** (ὅσιος), which means not a profane man, but religious, devout, and pious towards God and His sacred worship. Also, as ἐγκρατῆς, **self-controlled**, one who can restrain and subdue the desires of the flesh so that they do not erupt into vices that would besmirch the ministry.

And thus far, he has indeed proposed the type of a Bishop, what and how he should be in conversation, life, and morals. Now he paints the other part of this ideal, and shows how he should conduct himself in doctrine and in his teaching role; namely, to be **holding fast to the trustworthy word as he has been taught**. He describes the Word of God with a kind of periphrasis, calling it πιστὸν λόγον, not only because it surpasses the grasp of reason, to be more "trustworthy" (πιστὸς) than "understandable" (νοητὸς), but also because it is a certain, faithful, and undoubted Word with respect to its Author; namely, spoken from the mouth of God, and therefore worthy of faith, to be religiously accepted in faith. And he writes that this word is **according to the teaching**; that is, so arranged that it can usefully teach men to confirm faith, nourish piety, and rightly set up ways of life, indeed even to be instructed for eternal life. Therefore, he wants the Bishop to be **holding fast** to this **faithful word**, so that neither by the deceit of Satan does he allow it to be snatched from his heart and opinions contrary to the truth to be instilled, nor in seeking the favor of men does he reject the truth, or out of fear of them change or suppress anything, and thus betray or conceal the truth before his listeners; but he should steadfastly profess it from the Sacred Scripture.

Furthermore, he must be **able to exhort through sound doctrine**; that is, be endowed with this necessary gift to persuasively and effectively encourage his listeners toward every act of piety and righteousness, and this not through trivial and old wives' tales, nor through empty human inventions, but **through sound doctrine**, so that true things correspond to true things, and he does not try to deter people from sinning and encourage them to do good through falsehoods.

Thirdly, **that he may be able to refute those who contradict**, meaning that he should be able to refute and rebuke those who oppose and contradict the truth of heavenly doctrine, using the Word of God. In this way, he can not only present sound and uncorrupted doctrine in a positive assertion (Thesis) but also refute corruptions and errors in a contrasting argument (Antithesis) based on the foundation of the Holy Scriptures.

Common Places.

First. We are taught at the beginning that the matters pertaining to the state of the Church cannot all be organized simultaneously and at once, especially when a Church is newly planted. Moreover, the Church is so arranged that it always needs correction and improvement: this is due to the stumbling blocks that are presented at any time, either in doctrine or in life, just as in the external temple of Jerusalem, from time to time, those parts that were in ruins needed to be restored (as is apparent from the books of Kings). This point is made evident by the example of the churches that Paul planted, such as the Corinthian, Galatian, etc. Thus, this work is never so completely finished in this life that ministers may rightfully rest on their laurels, turn a deaf ear, and celebrate holidays. But time and again, even in well-established churches, there are things to be corrected, improved, and changed for the better. This calls for the diligence of the ministers of the Word.

Second. It is also noteworthy that Paul appoints Titus as the General Superintendent of the Cretan churches, to ensure that everything in the churches is done correctly and decently, to appoint other Bishops, and to diligently inquire into their teaching and life. From this, it is clear that God does not approve of anarchy (ἀναρχία) in the ecclesiastical ministry, which would be the mother of all disorder (ἀταξίας) and turmoil. Instead, He requires that there be a certain order among the ministers themselves, with different levels and ranks, so that, by the diversity of gifts, some preside and others are subordinate. This order was not recently introduced but has been accepted in the Church since the time of the Apostles. Indeed, God Himself, with His diverse gifts, distinguished among ministers and established ranks. According to this: "When He ascended on high, He gave gifts to men, and He gave some as Apostles, others as Prophets, others as Evangelists, others as Pastors and Teachers, for the equipping of the saints, for the work of ministry, for the edification of the body of Christ" (Ephesians 4).

Third. Meanwhile, the words of the Apostle do not establish that primacy of power which the Roman Pontiff claims for himself, defining it as the authority to decree in matters of religion according to his own will, and also the full use of both the spiritual and temporal swords. This kind of primacy the Lord repeatedly forbade to His disciples when they argued about primacy: "The kings of the Gentiles lord it over them; and those who exercise authority over them call themselves Benefactors. But you are not to be like that." [Mat. 20] "The greatest among you should be like the youngest, and the one who rules like the one who serves." [Luke 22] "Do not be called Rabbi: for one is your Master, even Christ; and all ye are brethren" (Matthew 23). And far from that praetorian power and dictatorial authority to decree and determine anything, even contrary to the Epistles of Paul (as the Pope has arrogated to himself without any shame or piety), being consonant with the Word of God, it is rather to be regarded as a principal mark and great sign of the Antichrist coming into the world, which Paul most clearly teaches by the Holy Spirit (2 The. 2).

Fourth. On the distinction between the function of the Apostles and other ministers in the Church. The Apostles were not assigned a specific parish, village, city, province, etc., but the whole world was their parish, according to this: "Go into all the world and preach the Gospel to every creature." All other ministers are assigned a specific boundary, a designated place within which they should confine themselves to the preaching of the Word and the administration of the Sacraments, and not intrude elsewhere, unless they are legitimately called either to perform said ministerial duties or to institute some Reformation. Thus, a Bishop or Superintendent has his specific diocese; a Pastor his church; just as Paul instructs Titus to appoint Presbyters in every town. However, Scripture does not forbid a Pastor to educate the Church of God through public writings (if he possesses that gift) or to refute heretics proliferating elsewhere. In a common cause, the Teachers of the Churches are bound to join their efforts, who otherwise, outside such a case, focus their care on the particular church entrusted to them, just as each head of a household [*paterfamilias*], outside of common danger, cares for his own house, but in a city fire or other public danger, everyone runs to help and joins their efforts to avert it.

Fifth is about the calling of ministers to teach the Word of God. Rightly does St. Paul elsewhere write: "Whoever aspires to the office of Bishop desires a noble task." [1 Timothy 3] Therefore, offering one's service to the Church is allowed and permissible. However, to intrude oneself by illegitimate means and to perform ministerial duties without an ordinary calling is not permissible. "No one takes this honor on himself; he must be called by God, just as Aaron was." [Hebrews 5] Now, ministers are called by God not as the Prophets and Apostles were called immediately, but those who are called by the voice and suffrage [*voce et suffragio*] of the Church enjoy a legitimate and truly divine calling, although it is mediated. A very clear example of this is provided by the present passage of the Apostle, recognizing as legitimately called those whom Titus was appointing in each town to the Churches. And in Acts 20, he says that the Presbyters of the Church of Ephesus were appointed as Bishops by the Holy Spirit, even though they were not called directly by God or Christ, but were ordained by the Apostles or their disciples. Just as Sosthenes, Timothy, Silvanus, etc., whom he includes as his colleagues in the subscriptions of his letters, he proclaims as servants of Jesus Christ, although they were called, not immediately, but mediately. Therefore, those who are called in this way through the suffrage of the Church today and are confirmed in the ministry by the authority of the Presbytery should have no doubt that they are divinely called. Relying on their calling, they can overcome, with God's help, any adversities and temptations in the ministry thrown against them by Satan and the World, which otherwise overwhelm those who remember that they have intruded themselves into this sacred and arduous office by evil means, and have run without being called.

Sixth. {On the Right to Call Ministers.} However, a question arises here for discussion; namely, in whose hands today rests the right to call ministers. It is evident from the present passage that neither did the Apostle impose Titus upon the unwilling Church of Crete, nor did Titus appoint Bishops or Pastors to the town churches without their consent. Therefore, in the calling of Ministers, the suffrage not only of the Bishops, but also of the Church is required, to which, if it has just reasons for refusing someone, Preachers should not be imposed against its will. And it is very wrong if either a Bishop seizes all that right (which is common to the Church) for himself alone, as the Roman Pontiff has done and does through tyranny, or if the Magistrate, without consulting the Ministry and against the justifiable refusal of the Church, forcibly imposes whoever he pleases. Just as there are three distinct orders in the Church (namely the Presbytery, the Magistrate, and the people), so in calling Ministers, the votes of all three orders should be joined together in their own distinct way and reason. The people judge life and morals, and also to some extent the gift of teaching. The Presbytery or the Church Council [*Senatus Ecclesiasticus*] inquires into the gifts particular to the ministry, whether someone is sound in doctrine, holds to the pattern of sound words, is didactic, and equipped with other necessary gifts for teaching. The Magistrate, in turn, governs the matter with its authority, ensuring that everything is conducted legitimately.

{No one should be imposed on the people if they have justifiable reasons for refusal.}

To speak specifically about each order, starting with the laity, which is the largest part of the Church and hence often comes under the name and appellation of the Church itself: It is certainly clear that they should not be deprived of this right [of refusal], as the following reasons most clearly demonstrate.

1. Firstly, what concerns all orders in the Church should rightly be agreed upon by all. But the appointment of sound and suitable ministers affects all orders, and therefore also primarily the laity, which encompasses the largest and most significant part of the Church. Therefore, no one should be imposed upon the laity if

they are unwilling or have justifiable reasons for rejecting someone.

2. Then it is evident by the authority of the Apostle Paul, who in a matter far lesser (e.g., the collection of alms) does not select persons without the Church's vote, but expressly writes: "whom you approve by your letters, them I will send." [1 Cor. 16] Hence, we can argue from the lesser to the greater: If in a much lesser matter, concerning only temporal things, the Apostle decidedly thought that the Church's opinion should be heard, and those should be sent whom the Church of Corinth would approve and specifically designate—how much more in the greatest of all matters (which involves the preservation of the divine service, the purity of doctrine, the consciences of people, and consequently the eternal salvation of the Church) should it be done in accordance with the consent and will of the Church, and thus also of the laity, or at least of those who in a pure Church represent the laity and are joined in the fellowship of faith to the Church they represent.

3. The utmost fairness of the matter itself teaches and demands the same. Are not preachers "ministers of the Church"? Indeed, the Church is the mistress, holding the keys in the house of God, of which ministers not lords but heralds of the Word. Hence, everyone should consider this: If in human affairs a matron in her own house were deprived of her right to hire servants, and if servants were imposed on her without consultation and against her will, those in whom she did not consent, would not everyone cry out that it is most unjust? And who then, of sound mind, could approve if, in the house of God, namely the Church, ministers are forcibly imposed on the mistress of the household, whom she herself does not choose or approve with her own voice?

4. The same conclusion is also drawn from the article of the Creed in which we profess to believe in the communion of saints. Among these goods that are proper to the Church, the ministry

and the adamant [ἀδαμαντίνως] right to call ministers are included, which is more evident than needing proof. Therefore, whoever deprives the Church of the right of ministry, to which the calling infallibly belongs, robs it of its own goods and violently disrupts and uproots that communion of saints.

5. Moreover, since Saint Paul requires that a Bishop or Pastor have a good testimony from those who are outside, to whom he is not appointed, how much more is the approval of the Church to which he is appointed, and which has a great interest in what kind of Pastor it has, required for his ordinary calling?

6. Additionally, the practice of the holy Apostles and the early Church contributes to this understanding. For in the choosing of Matthias, the Apostles sought the consent of the Church, as is clearly related in Acts 1. And the fact that this calling was divinely governed in an extraordinary manner does not detract from our purpose; rather, it strongly confirms what we intend. Indeed, if the Apostles did not want that calling, which God Himself wondrously directed, to take place without the approval and consent of the Church, even though it seemed that God's governance alone would have been sufficient to confer authority and to legitimize the calling even without the people's approval, how much less should the Church's consensus be neglected in a calling that lacks such extraordinary governance? So that what is lacking authority from an extraordinary miracle is supplemented by the ordinary suffrage and testimony of the Church. And if the Apostles (who, as unquestionable servants of God, seemed to be sufficient in their own Apostolic authority to establish a legitimate calling) still did not want to carry out this matter without the Church's suffrage: How much less should those, whose authority is not as great as that of the Apostles, call and ordain ministers without the consent of the Church? Nor does it hinder us that then they were consulting about choosing an Apostle, whereas today it is about calling

ordinary ministers. For the difference in order does not create a diversity in the ministry itself, which is and remains God's ministry, whether conducted by Apostles, or by Pastors and Deacons, and for whose administration a legitimate calling of Pastors or Deacons, approved by the Church's vote, is required, just as in the Apostles.

Furthermore, when the early Church was about to choose Deacons (who, besides the economic administration of goods, sometimes also preached, as is evident from the example of Stephen), the Apostles did not want to do anything without consulting the Church. Instead, they sought the voice and testimony of the Church, as is clearly read in Acts 6. If anyone objects that the Church's suffrage was especially sought because these Deacons were to manage matters pertaining to its sustenance, this does not fully address the issue. Besides the fact that these Deacons took on some part of the ministry of the Word, the objection can also be inverted in this way: If the Apostles recognized it as just and fair that the Church should decide who should be the caretakers of its temporal goods, whether they were suitable or not, then how much more does fairness dictate that the Church should know who will be the caretakers and dispensers of its heavenly treasures—whether they are faithful and suitable for such a significant task? Since they are entrusted not with temporal goods, but with those riches on which the salvation of souls hinges and turns.

But let us proceed to show the practice of the holy Apostles and the early Church. When the Church in Jerusalem heard the news that a great number of Greeks or Gentiles in Antioch had converted to God, the early Christian Church sent Barnabas to go to Antioch to strengthen them. Here again, it is demonstrated more clearly than the sun that the Church should not be deprived of its right to call Ministers. A similar case is recorded in Acts 15, where, following a dispute over the necessity of circumcision, the

Christians of the Antioch Church decided to send Paul and Barn-abas, along with some others, up to Jerusalem to the Synod of the Apostles and Presbyters. And towards the end of that synodal dis-cussion, it reads: "it seemed good to the Apostles and Presbyters, with the whole CHURCH, to choose men from among them and send them to Antioch, to convey the decrees of the Apostolic Syn-od to the Antioch Church." In Acts 14, Paul and Barnabas are said to have appointed Presbyters in each Church BY SUFFRAGE. Therefore, the Apostles, although notable for their high authority, deemed that in matters concerning the public good of the Church, especially in the calling and sending of Ministers, nothing should be done without the approval of the Church.

From this, Cyprian in Book 1, Letter 3, testifies that a Bish-op appointed in place of one deceased was chosen by the unan-imous suffrage of the people. And in Letter 4, he says: "It is very appropriate to give the power either to choose priests or to reject the unworthy."

The example of Saint Ambrose is also well known, how he was elected Bishop by the unanimous voice of the people. And the Council of Carthage decreed that Bishops, Priests, and Clergy as ministers of the Churches should not be ordained unless there is the consent of the clergy and the people. This statute and canon are frequently mentioned in the said council.

And even if in this matter, in terms of appearance, the same form was not always observed, yet in terms of its essence, it has been a perpetual custom that no one should ever be appointed to the Ministry against the will and refusal of the congregation, but rather their suffrage in naming individuals or their approval in con-firming those already nominated was required.

However, since the entire multitude of the people cannot always be involved in the deliberation to avoid confusion, it is not inappropriate that in some places the people delegate their voting power and authority to the Magistrate, who is a fellow adherent of the same confession and doctrine, or confer their right on certain more honorable persons who represent the people, without whose consent the calling is not legitimate. Even so, the rest of the people or the congregation of the Church are not completely deprived of their right; if they reject someone for plausible reasons, this just refusal must be respected, and another person should be appointed, to whom such a prestigious office can rightly be entrusted without just complaint. And this concerns the people.

{The judgment of the Presbytery is required for the calling of Ministers.}

Furthermore, these following reasons infallibly teach that legitimate calling cannot be separated from the consent of the Presbytery. First, there is an unchanging rule: Careful consideration must be taken not to call the unworthy or unfit to the ministry, but rather a judgment should first be made of their gifts—whether they are pure in doctrine, hold the mystery of faith, adhere to the form of sound words, are capable of teaching, can rightly divide the word of God, exhort through sound doctrine, and refute those who contradict—as Paul expressly requires all these qualities in a minister of the Word, when in his letters to Timothy and Titus, he instructs that a thorough inquiry and examination into the gifts of those being called to the Ministry be conducted (1 Timothy 3, Titus 1).

Regarding these gifts, no one can judge more quickly or decide more correctly than theologians who are practiced in all aspects of the ecclesiastical ministry and have acquired from God's Word the knowledge by which they can judge such important matters. Therefore, to them is chiefly entrusted the judgment of doctrine and other necessary gifts, which should not be neglected in the election of Pastors of the Church. Concerning this matter, there exist testimonies of the greatest weight in the Sacred Scriptures, as when the Apostle writes and instructs Titus to appoint Presbyters in every town, and he warns the same to repel Judaizing pseudo-apostles from the office of the Presbytery. When it is said to Timothy (a Bishop): "Do not be hasty in the laying on of hands, nor share in other people's sins." [1 Timothy 5] Similarly: "And the things that you have heard from me among many witnesses, commit these to faithful men who will be able to teach others also." [2 Timothy 2]

And again, the perpetual practice of the whole Church from the time of the Apostles shows that no calling of ministers was considered legitimate if it lacked the approval of the Presbytery, except in the sole case of necessity, when an adequate number of Presbyters could not be had. The Apostles performed their roles in the calling of Matthias, as well as in confirming the Deacons. Similarly, the teachers and prophets who were in Antioch were instructed to set apart Barnabas and Saul for the work of the Ministry, whom they also, after solemn prayers, confirmed for that calling through the laying on of hands. Thus, Paul and Barnabas appointed Presbyters in Iconium, Lystra, and Antioch. Timothy was confirmed for the Ministry by the authority of the Presbytery, 1 Timothy 4. Along with these testimonies of the Sacred Scriptures and the examples of the Apostles, the canons of the Councils of Nicaea, Carthage, and others concur, where the judgment, examination, and suffrage of the Presbytery are given primary roles in the calling of ministers.

{Regarding the calling of Ministers, the vote of a FAITHFUL Magistrate is necessary.}

Finally, concerning the Magistrate: Their vote should not be neglected either—provided that they are faithful and committed to the Christian religion. Indeed, in the early days of the Church, when the Magistrate was alien to the faith of the Gospel, they had no role in the election of ministers, nor any suffrage. The Apostles would not have allowed the judgment regarding the appointment of ministers to fall to a profane Magistrate, to whom Paul does not even want disputes about matters concerning temporal sustenance to be deferred (as in 1 Corinthians 6), much less matters pertaining to the Church's ministry. Later, however, when the Magistrate embraced the Christian religion, their authority was also applied and required in the calling of ministers. But as time progressed, the Roman Bishops, through tyranny, seized this right for themselves alone, excluding the Magistrate, as if their vote was unnecessary, as is known from history, and the impious canon of the Council of Trent exists on this matter, chapter 4, "Concerning the Sacrament of Orders."

However, it should not be overlooked that the judgment of a faithful and Christian Magistrate is clearly evident from the books of Kings and Chronicles, with examples of Jehoshaphat, Hezekiah, and Josiah, who took great care to abolish idolatry and restore the pure worship of God, removing idolatrous priests and appointing and ordaining others in their place. Yet, they did not administer all these things by themselves alone, but did so with the authority of the Presbytery, that is, either of the pious priests or certainly of the prophets, who exhorted the restoration of sincere worship and piously moderated it with their salutary counsels.

Moreover, just as a faithful Magistrate has its roles, its desire [*suum votum*], and authority in the governance of the calling of ministers, so, too, must it never neglect the judgment of the Presbytery; that is, those who by reason of their office ought and can judge the gifts necessary and proper for the ministry.

Therefore, the insistence of certain magnates or even some

nobles cannot be approved, who often, without consulting those [Presbyters] (whose office requires them to judge the gifts of those to be ordained), appoint church ministers of their own choosing, and seize for themselves alone that right which is common to the Church.

It is also discerned from this, what should be established according to the Word of God, if in some place (where the free exercise of sincere religion is allowed by public sanction of religious peace[1]) a Pontifical Magistrate nonetheless transfers the entire right of appointing ministers to Evangelical Churches to himself alone. For it has already been shown with the strongest demonstrations that such a calling cannot be considered legitimate if it lacks either the approval of the Church to which the minister is to be appointed, or the vote and judgment of the Presbytery. And since even a Magistrate who professes himself in doctrinal agreement (ὁμόψηφον) with the Church seeking a minister is not allowed this, how much less will it be permitted to Magistrates who profess a different religion, especially in places where churches embracing the Augsburg Confession should be left free to exercise their religion according to the sacred constitution of public peace? Particularly when the right of calling ministers is not counted among political regalia but pertains to ecclesiastical administration, which all of sound judgment recognize should not be confused with political governance. And how can such Magistrates appoint ministers of a different religion to those churches, of which they do not acknowledge themselves as members, while, at the same time, excluding the consent and approval of those very churches and their members? Would this not be mixing heaven with earth, and inverting the nature of things? Surely the Church which is concerned, will be excluded from the right of calling its own ministers, while others,

1 Hunnius wrote in the context of the Peace of Augsburg (1555), which established the legal status of the Church of the Augsburg Confession.

completely foreign to that Church in terms of faith, will impose on it ministers of their own choosing? Thus, strangers (who are neither members nor wish to be called as such) will rule in the house of Evangelical Churches, while the actual members are excluded and deprived of their rights. Furthermore, since Pontifical Magistrates do not even have the right to appoint priests to their own churches (as all such authority is arrogated by the Pope and his Bishops), how much less power will they have to impose Ministers on unwilling Evangelical Churches? Can a Magistrate have more power in a Church of which he is not a member than in one of which he acknowledges and professes himself a partner? And with what conscience can such a Magistrate ordain ministers of another religion, from which he himself is completely alienated and separated?

Paul, when explicitly describing how those aspiring to ecclesiastical office should be prepared, among other characteristics, places this as particularly notable and memorable: That they should be capable of refuting and convincing those who contradict. But I ask you, do you believe that a Pontifical Magistrate, who wholeheartedly abhors the Evangelical doctrine of our churches, would appoint ministers to the Churches of the Augsburg Confession who are able to powerfully refute those contradicting the truth? Would they not rather appoint those who either cannot—or are not supposed to, according to directive—criticize or refute the manifold idolatry, abuses, superstitions, and horrendous errors of Romanism with the necessary zeal and gravity, which are in conflict with the very foundation of the salvation of souls? How, then, can the calling be legitimate, where that Apostolic Canon about calling those who can silence the contradicting is deliberately neglected and disregarded? This is most firmly demonstrated by the end and purpose of the Ordinary Calling [Ordinariae Vocationis], which is demanded by the Word of God and desired by the Church to which the called [minister] is to be appointed. For since the calling should align with this aim and end, that the Word of the Gospel may spread, that the sound doctrine we hold may be propagated, and thereby the Evangelical Church associated with the Augsburg Confession may gain strength and growth: Who would be so incredibly foolish as to expect this end from the adversaries professedly against the Gospel and sound doctrine we embrace, and not rather an entirely opposite and very different end? How, then, can such a calling be ordinary and valid before God? And how can sincere Teachers, to whom the orthodox religion is dear, consent to such a calling, since it is clearer than daylight from the presented reasons that it is not legitimate? By what right would such Pastors run, not called, nor entering the sheepfold through the true door, but breaking in from elsewhere—because they are neither called directly by God, nor indirectly through the voice of the Church and the authority of the Presbytery, as Paul speaks, but hired by those who, neither being members nor partners in the confession of the true doctrine of the Church of God, can hardly represent the Church. Therefore, those hired could not be said to be called by the CHURCH.

And this is also entirely the opinion of Martin Luther. He indeed assigns roles to the Magistrate who embraces the sincere doctrine of the Gospel in the calling of ministers. But where has he ever conceded this to a PONTIFICAL Magistrate who is alien to the doctrine of our churches?—Much less to grant full authority to act at will in the appointment of ministers and to impose on Evangelical Churches Preachers of their own choosing?

Luther never thought or judged that this right should be absolutely conceded to even an orthodox Magistrate, excluding the Presbytery and the approval of the people. For in Volume 6 of the Jena edition, page 352, published in 1568, in a letter to a certain parish priest, he very clearly and expressly advises that it is not permissible for a senate or city to dismiss any Preacher or minister of the Church, or even a Superintendent of a school, or to receive and impose another in place of the dismissed, without the knowledge and against the will of the parish priest of that place, whose vote, will, and consent the senate cannot neglect in this matter, unless it wants to confuse political administration with ecclesiastical.

Luther also grants this through a certain conditional concession, not a simple one, that Bishops may remain Bishops, if either they themselves perform their duties properly, or, because of their inexperience, they are unable to properly fulfill their duties, at least they appoint others who are capable and suitable for teaching, just as Valerius, when hindered in teaching by the faculty of speech, appointed Saint Augustine in his place. By "suitable," Luther understands those who teach the Gospel sincerely, and as he himself explicitly discusses their duty elsewhere, who strongly and powerfully CONDEMN the PAPACY as the kingdom of Satan. Such teachers, however, cannot be obtained or expected from Pontifical Bishops, as long as they continue to be Pontifical.

Although Luther also writes that some secular Magistrates, Senators, and Princes hired Preachers of their own choosing with a fixed salary, without any permission from Bishops and Pontiffs, he intended this only in the case of necessity, which he discusses there. This is because, especially at the beginning of the reestablished teaching of the Gospel, they could not obtain sincere ministers from the Pontifical Bishops, who had degenerated into wolves, and it was neither fair nor advisable for their own salvation to be completely devoid of ministry. In such a case, they did rightly in contracted for themselves learned and pious ministers with their own stipends, without waiting for or requiring the suffrage of the PONTIFICAL Bishops. For why should it not be permissible in such a case for either the magistracy or the people, and thus the Church, to call Ministers, even when no Presbytery has yet been established—and thus to newly establish a Presbytery, whose subsequent knowledge, consent, judgment, and approval would be used to call suitable Ministers?

Thus, Luther is addressing the case of necessity there and speaks of a non-Pontifical, but Evangelical Magistrate. Indeed, he grants the Evangelical Magistrate the power to call Evangelical Ministers, but not absolutely without the consent of the Presbytery, except in the case when no pure Presbytery has yet been established. And to summarize, wherever Dr. Luther mentions the calling of Evangelical Ministers and assigns it in part to the Magistrate, he always speaks of the Evangelical Magistrate, not the Pontifical one, which is important to note carefully. Whenever he also, through concession, grants some right in this matter to Pontifical Bishops, he always does so under such a condition that neither the Bishops nor others of any Pontifical order will ever fulfill; namely, that they appoint sincere and suitable people who refute errors in doctrine and, in particular, strongly condemn the Papacy as the kingdom of Satan.

But as for the opinion that this power should be granted to Pontifical Bishops, either without this express condition or even without the consent of the people, not only can this not be demonstrated from any testimony of Luther, but the contrary is evident in his treatise where he explains the reasons why it is lawful for the Christian Church to inquire into the teachings of its ministers. There {Volume 2 of the Jena edition.} he writes: "If today's Bishops and Abbots occupied the seat of the Apostles, as they boast, then indeed it might be allowed for them to do what Titus, Timothy, Paul, and Barnabas did in the ordination of ministers. But since they occupy the seat of the devil and are wolves who neither want to teach nor tolerate the Gospel, therefore the ordination of the ministry and the care of souls among Christians pertains to them no more than to Turks and Jews. The care of donkeys and dogs should have been entrusted to them. Moreover, even if they were true Bishops who wanted to have the Gospel and ordain true Preachers, they could not and should not do so without the will, election, and calling of the Church."

From these, it is clear what the perpetual and consistent opinion of Doctor Luther is regarding the ordinary calling [*Ordinaria vocatione*], which must be carried out with the will, consent, and approval of the persons in the Church if it is to be considered legitimate and ordinary. And let this suffice to be said about the right of calling the ministers of the Word, occasioned by the Apostolic text. Let us proceed to the articles of doctrine or Common Places remaining to be observed from this part of the Chapter.

Seventh. Therefore, the seventh place is about the life and conduct of the ministers of the Word, which according to Saint Paul's Canon should be holy and blameless. Indeed, it holds great weight and significance if a minister of the Church not only exhorts his listeners to piety through words, but also presents a good example to them through the integrity of life and innocence of manners, like a light and torch. As Paul advises in 1 Timothy 3, a Bishop or Preacher of the Word must have a good reputation among outsiders to avoid disgrace and the snares of the slanderer. And in 1 Timothy 4: "Be an example to the believers in word, in conduct, in love, in spirit, in faith, in purity." And in Titus 2: "In all things show yourself to be a pattern of good works; in doctrine showing integrity, reverence, incorruptibility, sound speech that cannot be condemned." Such a life of ministers builds up the Church of God no less than the exhortation of doctrine. Therefore, Saint Paul often presents the example of his own conduct to Christians, as in 1 Corinthians 4 and 11 and Philippians 3. On the contrary, how indecent it is before God and the holy angels if those who should have been examples of all sanctity defile themselves with vices? Can it not rightly be said to them:

"Physician, heal thyself"? And that saying of the wise man: "It is shameful for a teacher, when his own fault reproves him"? Indeed, such a minister of the Church dictates rules of living to others but does not keep to the path of his own life; he prescribes to others to observe God's commands, yet himself shows them the middle finger; he imposes burdens on others, which he himself does not touch even with the smallest finger (Matthew 23). As opposed to the teachers of the Jewish people, Paul thundered in a grave sermon: "You who teach another, do you not teach yourself? You who preach that one should not steal, do you steal? You who say, do not commit adultery, do you commit adultery? You who abhor idols, do you commit sacrilege? You who boast in the law, through breaking the law, do you dishonor God?" (Romans 2). And since the Lord threatens eternal woe to anyone who offends even one of the least, what punishment, then, should be expected for those who offend not one, not two, not a few, but the whole Church, to whom it was fitting, by reason of their office, to shine before others in the sincerity of doctrine and the holiness of life?

Eighth. On the marriage of Priests or Ministers of the Church. Here we have not a human testimony, but a divine one from the Holy Spirit himself, who through the mouth and pen of the Apostle Paul ordained that a Bishop should be the husband of one wife. St. Paul almost repeats verbatim this Orthodox and Apostolic Canon in the third chapter of his first letter to Timothy. From this, it is clear how great is the impiety of the Pontifical Doctors, who prefer to use manifest violence against the testimony of their own conscience and the words of the Apostle, rather than to recant and abandon their palpable and clearly exposed error and demonic doctrine, as the Apostle names it. They claim that no one living in marriage should be tolerated or admitted to ecclesiastical ministry, and they insinuate that their priests commit a lesser sin if they keep ten concubines at home than if they have one legitimate wife. Is this not spitting on God's most sacred ordinance with the filthiest of mouths, and trampling it underfoot with wicked feet? Just as, with equal impiety, the Roman Pontiff in his so-called Canon Law dared to use Paul's words to justify the impure celibacy: "Those who are in the flesh cannot please God," as if to brand the eternal God, the author of marriage, with the mark of shame, and to denounce sacred marriage with the black mark of damnation—thus declaring himself the Antichrist to the whole world. For Paul, inspired by the Holy Spirit, prophesied of his kingdom, that in the latter times there would come deceitful teachers, heeding seducing spirits and doctrines of devils, speaking lies in hypocrisy, having their conscience seared with a hot iron, forbidding to marry, and commanding to abstain from meats, which God hath created to be received with thanksgiving by those who believe. How can that man, the son of sin and eternal damnation, dare to assert that those who live in marriage live in the flesh and cannot please God? Were not the holy patriarchs, who were all husbands, living in the flesh and not pleasing to God? Did not Enoch, who begot sons and daughters in marriage and walked with God, live in the flesh and not please Him? {Genesis 5} This is the same Enoch who is remembered in the Sacred Scriptures as one of the foremost heralds of righteousness in the original world. Did Abraham, Isaac, Jacob, Joseph, Moses, and countless other saints, while living in marriage, live in the flesh in such a way that they could not please God? What of the high priest of the Old Testament, or the other priests, to whom it was said: "Be holy, for I am holy."? Were they not also married, yet did not live in the desires of the flesh, but pleased God through faith? God Himself defined by express law what kind of wives they should take into the covenant of marriage. {Leviticus 21} And is it right for this Roman Antichrist to condemn the Apostles with his wicked decrees? For Paul explicitly writes that they had wives and took them along with them in their apostleship. Thus, St. Paul says: "Do we not have the right to take along a believing wife, as do the other Apostles and the Lord's brothers and Cephas [Peter]?" {1 Corinthians 9} They cannot escape by interpreting "sisters, a wife" as concubines. For who is so profane and impious as to think that the most holy servants of God, the Apostles, kept concubines rather than legitimately led around their wives?

From all of these things, those who are not struck by a fatal stupor, blindness, and madness of heart can see how much value should be placed on that donkey-like evasion and quibbling of the Papists, who claim to have cut all the sinews of the Apostle's testimony when they twist Paul's words in this way: "A Bishop must be the husband of one wife," meaning, the Bishop of only one church. First, is it permissible to call the Church the wife of a Bishop, and the Bishop the husband of the Church? Is this not a slap in the face to the Apostle Paul, who recognizes only ONE Husband for the Church? The Church, I say, not only universal (of which the Roman Bishop boasts himself as the spouse) but also particular, such as the Church of the Corinthians, to whom he writes these words: "I promised you to one husband, to Christ, so that I might present you as a pure virgin to Him." {2 Corinthians 11} Therefore, not even John the Baptist, who (besides the Savior, Christ) no greater has been born of women, dared to call himself the husband of the Church, or to name it his bride or wife. But removing all such praise from himself, he transferred it uniquely to Christ, saying, "The one who has the bride is the bridegroom." {John 3} How beautifully, then, the falsification of the Papists stands, who prefer to make any—even the most impure—priests, to the disgrace of Christ, the husbands and spouses of the churches, and to twist the words of the Holy Spirit against their conscience, rather than to attribute the praise of truth to the most illustrious testimony of Paul about the marriage of Bishops, and to acknowledge and correct their Antichristian doctrine? What about Paul's statement in 1 Timothy 3, which clearly refutes that distortion, when he not only joins a wife to the Bishop or Pastor, but also adds: "He must manage his own family well and see that his children obey him, and he must do so in a manner worthy of full respect. (If anyone does not know how to manage his own family, how can he take care of God's Church?)" Here he explicitly states that he is joining a wife to the Bishop, with whom he may have children and establish his own household, which is distinct from the Church over which he presides, so that a judgment can be made from the management of his family, wife, and children as to whether he is suitable for governing the Church. If he cannot manage his own family and children, much less can he be set over the Church of God. All of these things, while they affirm the marriage of church ministers as consistent with the Word of God, also completely overturn the demonic doctrine of the Antichristian kingdom about the prohibition of marriage.

Ninth. On the discipline of the families of Preachers, which must be precise because of the example set. Therefore, Paul so carefully advises that Bishops should have well- and liberally-educated children. It cannot be said how much of a stumbling block it is if either the wives or children of the ministers of the Word are poorly behaved, infamous for vices and scandals, just as the impropriety of Eli's sons offended all of Israel and brought great contempt upon the sacrifices. Similarly, God ordained in explicit law concerning the daughter of a Priest, that if she begins to prostitute herself, she shall be burned, adding the reason: because she has dishonored her father (Leviticus 21).

Tenth. On the majesty of ecclesiastical ministry, where the Teachers of the Church are called stewards of God. It is a great honor and dignity to be an official of any monarch. Such offices are only entrusted to honored persons. How much more august, then, is it to be the steward of God Himself, or an official in His house? Therefore, to assert the dignity of the Church's ministry, St. Paul says: "Let a man so account of us, as of the ministers of Christ, and stewards of the mysteries of God" (1 Corinthians 4). This should instill in listeners a reverence for such a holy office, and consequently for the persons placed in it, so they do not regard and scoff at teachings as mere human notions when ministers teach, reprove, or exhort from the Lord's Word. It should also arouse ministers to careful and diligent care, as they are entrusted not with earthly goods, but with the mysteries of God, in whose knowledge lies the salvation of souls. They should remember to handle these mysteries in a holy and religious manner, and to dispense them in such a way that as many as possible are gained for Christ and are eternally saved. And they should consider that they will one day give a most serious account of their administered office, as taught by the Holy Spirit in Ezekiel 33, 1 Peter 5, and Christ in the parables of Matthew 25, Luke 12, and 16.

Eleventh. It is also apparent from the words of the Apostle that the Bishops, of whom he indeed speaks here, differ in no way in office from the Presbyters. For, having previously instructed to appoint Presbyters in every town, he then, to show how they should be constituted, adds: "For a Bishop must be blameless, etc." Therefore, it is a tyranny in the Church of God that should not be tolerated, that the name of Bishop has been seized by those who are not Presbyters or Ministers of the Church (but princes of this world) and who do not perform any duties specific to the ministry, nor preach, nor dispense the Sacraments. Instead, they do much greater things (namely), they keep dogs and horses and exercise a principal and almost regal dominion, forgetting what Christ said: "The kings of the Gentiles exercise lordship over them, and those in authority over them are called benefactors (*Gnädige Herrn*); but you shall not be so" (Luke 22).

Twelfth. Let all Christians, each and every one, earnestly strive to flee and avoid the vices that Paul removes from the Bishops of the churches. Although they sometimes observe these faults in their ministers, they should not imitate the vices of their teachers, but their teaching and sound exhortation according to the standard of the Word. Nor should they think themselves excused before God by the example of their Pastors. {Luke 6.} Just as if a blind man leads a blind man, both will fall into a pit, so too, he who emulates the life of his preachers will receive judgment along with them.

Thirteenth. On the avoidance of Ἀυθάδεια, or arrogance and presumption, by which one thinks too highly of oneself, admires and exalts oneself alone. This Ἀυθάδεια is such a sin that it cast Satan out of the fellowship of the heavenly kingdom, when he, carried away by the admiration of his angelic excellence, despised the dominion of God the Creator. It is this same arrogance that produces so many heretics, who, once they have conceived an opinion in their minds, cherish it so tenderly as if it were the offspring and birth of their own intellect, preferring to defend it at the cost of souls rather than yield to celestial truth. Saint Paul proposes a remedy for this vice when he writes: "I say through the grace given to me to everyone among you, not to think of himself more highly than he ought to think, but to think with sober judgment" (Rom. 12).

Fourteenth. On avoiding Anger: Anger disrupts a person's ability to think and act prudently, soberly, and moderately, often leading to hasty actions that can put oneself and others in danger. James says, "Everyone should be quick to listen, slow to speak, and slow to become angry, for man's anger does not bring about the righteous life that God desires." Ecclesiastes also warns about this in chapter 7.

Fifteenth. Drunkenness, too, must be avoided by all the faithful, especially by the ministers of the churches. It conflicts with our very nature, which is usually satisfied with little. It goes against the commands of God, as noted in Luke 21 and Romans 13. And it leads to a great multitude of sins, as drunkenness is both the mother and the fuel of these vices. To rightly understand why Saint Paul associated drunkenness with ἀσωτίαν, which means all kinds of excess, debauchery, and intemperance, see Ephesians 5. This is in line with the warnings of the Holy Spirit found in Proverbs 20 and 23, Hosea 4, and Sirach 19 and 32. Therefore, the priests of the Old Testament were commanded by God to abstain from all intoxicating drink when performing sacred rites, as seen in Leviticus 10, to remind them of the importance of sobriety in such a venerable office. The grave judgment of God announced through Isaiah in chapters 28 and 56 came as a result of the Judean priests' neglect of this commandment.

Sixteenth. This passage teaches us that people who are martial in nature [*homines Martiales*], prone to fighting and striking, should not be chosen for the ministry of the Word. Their behavior can mar the ministry and often contributes little to edification. Ministers should be gentle, peaceable, and calm towards everyone, willing to teach, and patient with wrongdoers, treating them with gentleness and leniency. {2 Timothy 2.} For instance, Peter once took up the sword and cut off the ear of the high priest's servant, but he was admonished by Jesus to put his sword away, as those who live by the sword will die by it. The true weapons of ministers should be the Word of God, prayers, and tears, which are spiritual tools capable of withstanding not just the attacks of men but also all schemes and assaults of the devil. They can overcome anything that rises against Christ, as described in 2 Corinthians 10.

Seventeenth. This passage discusses greed and shameful gain-seeking (αἰσχροκερδεία), which, while destructive for all Christians as the root of all kinds of evil (1 Timothy 6), is especially intolerable in Teachers and Pastors of the Church of God. Greed turns a shepherd into a mercenary, motivated by base profit rather than a genuine calling, performing duties superficially and without true dedication, contrary to what Peter requires. Furthermore, for the sake of financial gain, such individuals are easily swayed in their doctrinal stance. They are unwilling to suffer the loss of material goods during times of persecution and will readily forsake the truth to preserve their wealth. The scandal caused by the avarice of Pastors among the congregation is also significant. Their corrupt examples are easily emulated, leading people to believe such behavior is permissible. It also gives rise to blasphemy against the ministry of the Word, as in the case of Eli's sons, Hophni and Phinehas, whose greed for portions of the sacrifices not rightfully theirs led to public disdain for the worship and sacrifices to God (1 Samuel 2).

Eighteenth. Consequently, it follows from this, and it is proven, that Pastors and Ministers of the Church must be supported with decent salaries, lest a window be opened to them for greed and base gain. For since they should, according to the Apostle's command, be devoted to reading (1 Timothy 4), not engage in manual trades, nor yet can they 'live on air,' as it is said, equity itself demands that (where there is not enough from ecclesiastical revenues for ministers to live on) a salary be established for them through a collection. For the laborer is worthy of his reward. {Matthew 10} And it is just that those who are instructed in all kinds of good things share them with those who instruct them {Galatians 6}, it is just that those who serve at the altar (should) partake of the altar, and those who proclaim the Gospel should live from the preaching of the Gospel (1 Corinthians 9). Just as the Lord formerly provided a very honorable salary for Priests and Levites (Leviticus 18), so would the temptation to greed and the desire for filthy lucre be cut off for ministers. So would they have the means to exercise hospitality, which Paul requires in a Bishop, both here and in 1 Timothy 3. So they could do good to strangers, exiles, and the poor. Lazy drones, monks, and priests, born to consume grain and drink wine with full throats in the realm of Antichrist, serving their only god, their belly, were once well-fed, although they neither served God nor men, but the devil and Antichrist, to the eternal destruction of souls. Now, however, this fountain of liberality has almost completely dried up towards the faithful servants of God and Preachers. But the Lord will no doubt avenge this ingratitude. Meanwhile, let the ministers of the Church console themselves with the much more noble reward laid up in heaven, which the Lord has promised to those who prove themselves fully in this office (Dan. 12, 1 Peter 5).

Nineteenth. The Apostle's requirement that a Bishop be "holding fast the faithful Word as he has been taught" serves as a reminder of steadfastness to all faithful teachers. They are not to abandon sound doctrine to curry favor with others, nor agree to such deceptive, ambiguous, and equivocal compromises under the attractive guise of peace which could undermine the truth. Instead, they should most resolutely defend the sacred trust of the Gospel doctrine, even unto death if necessary. They must remember that they are advocating not their own cause, but that of God. Thus, they should hold onto what they have, lest someone take their victory or crown from them {Revelation 2}. In this regard, they should not fear those who can kill the body, but not the soul {Matthew 10}. They must remain faithful unto death. If they preserve the purity of truth and the word of endurance, they, too, will be preserved from the hour of trial that is to come upon the whole world to test its inhabitants, as the Son of God promises with words of hope and consolation to the Angel or Pastor of the Church in Philadelphia (Revelation 3).

Twentieth. We are reminded that it is not enough for a Pastor to only teach doctrinal matters in the Church, that is, to present the doctrine of the articles of salvation from the pure sources of Israel, but it is also required that they exhort their people to every duty and piety. This is explicitly demanded by Saint Paul from the Pastors of the churches. Since Christianity is completed in these two aspects—to believe rightly and to live holy—a faithful Pastor will instruct the faith of their congregation by teaching the truth, and shape their lives by exhorting them towards righteousness and holiness. Just as Scripture itself is useful not only for teaching but also for exhortation (2 Timothy 3), Paul solemnly charges his Timothy to not only preach the Word but also to exhort and rebuke (2 Timothy 4).

Twenty-first. Since Paul wants this exhortation to be done through sound doctrine, we are taught that ministers should not base their exhortations on the fabled inventions of men, but on the solid Word of God. The Holy Spirit is not effective in planting piety in the hearts of listeners through lies or fables concocted by human ingenuity; these, like empty scarecrows, produce nothing but hypocrisy or some fear devoid of true piety of the soul. Just as the teachers of the Papal Kingdom tried to turn people to piety with nonsense about purgatory fire and other fables, and human traditions about the merit of good works, "They wanted to make people pious with lies." But the Holy Spirit is effective through His own instrument, which is the Word of God. This provides us with an immense ocean of sentences, parables, and examples for instituting salutary exhortations before the people. "They have Moses and the Prophets," says the Savior in the parable, "if they do not listen to these, they will not believe, even if someone should rise from the dead" (Luke 16).

Twenty-second. Among other characteristics of a true Bishop, Paul also assigns this one: That he should be able to convince those who contradict. Therefore, we are taught that it is not enough for someone to present the thesis and propose true and salutary doctrine; he must also press the antithesis: to refute and confute those who envelop heavenly doctrine in the clouds of errors and scatter teachings discordant with piety, striving to alienate the simple from the Shepherd of souls, Jesus Christ. These hostile wolves, who do not spare the flock, must be resisted at all costs, their sophistries must be unveiled, and the falsity of their opinions exposed so as not to deceive the less wary and cautious under the guise of truth. Thus, the Prophets, John the Baptist, Christ, the Apostles, and Teachers throughout all times have shut the mouths of those who contradict and have established significant antitheses, as evidenced by the entire volume of the Scriptures. This is a very necessary part of the pastoral office, as not everyone is saved in their own religion, but there is only one faith that saves; heresies, however, are among those sins that make a man an outcast from the kingdom of heaven (Galatians 5).

Twenty-third. From this, it also emerges that the teaching office should be entrusted to learned individuals who have acquired the ability from the Word of God to shut the mouths of those who contradict. Although in this, as in other aspects, the ministers of the churches are very unequal and not everyone is given the ability to dissolve all heretical sophistries, still, each Pastor is required to have such knowledge of theological matters that they can defend their flock from the incursions of wolves and demonstrate from the foundations of the Sacred Scriptures to their audience what is true, what is false, what should be held, and what should be rejected. And from the writings of sincere orthodox theologians, they should know how to confute, if not all, then at least the principal arguments of the opposing side. This is not only necessary because of the adversaries of truth, the heretics, but also, and especially in times of their silence, due to the tireless assaults of the devil. He suggests and instills various things to those who are tempted, to which those entrusted with the care of souls must be prepared and ready to respond, not only to men but also to shut the mouth of the devil himself, and so inform those who are tempted that they can shake off and extinguish the fiery darts of his temptation through the grace of God.

THIRD PART.

Up to this point, Paul has prescribed to Titus the form and ideal of a good and commendable Bishop, so that it would be clear what kind of men should have access to ecclesiastical functions. Now he clearly teaches which individuals he wants to be excluded from these functions. On this matter, the Apostle comments: **For there are many who are insubordinate**. He moves to a description of those whom he wants to be repelled from the office of teaching through an explanation. He explains the reason for his previous admonition, why it is necessary to institute a thorough examination and inquiry into the life, doctrine, and gifts of those who are called to govern the churches, and why they also should be powerful in refuting those who contradict. Because many who covet this office are in many ways unworthy and hence should be kept far away, such people, when teaching, should rather be contradicted by the Bishops and other Pastors, instead of wanting and desiring them to be admitted into the fellowship of the ministry. He calls these individuals ἀνθποτάκτους or **disobedient**, because they do not submit to true doctrine but actively and hostilely oppose it. He also labels them **empty talkers**, both because they declaim at length about trivial matters, incessantly inculcating their nonsense, neglecting necessary doctrine and exhortation without any benefit to their listeners, and because they impose vain doctrines as true upon the churches. The more sincere ministers in the Island of Crete should not overlook this, but should refute those false teachers and **shut their mouths** with Sacred Scripture.

Seducers of minds) Those who so blind the most noble power of the human soul (which ought to have been consecrated uniquely to God, truth, and the knowledge of the doctrine of faith) in their listeners, by casting the mists of human opinions, that they lead them astray from the path of truth, with their salvation at risk. He writes especially that they do this, **who are of the circumcision**, that is, those who, having become Christians from Jews, did not profess the doctrine of Christ sincerely, but foolishly mixed it with Jewish commentary, teaching that the salvation of man consists not only in faith in Christ, but also in the works of the Law, and that Circumcision is necessary for salvation.

Who overthrow whole houses, etc.) This is the reason explaining why these destructive wolves must be diligently refuted: Because they do not keep their false doctrines to themselves, but spread them among the common people and try to entangle unsuspecting and simple individuals with their snares—and, unfortunately, they have been all too successful. Indeed, they have **overthrown** entire **houses** or families with their most harmful errors, just as if someone were to shake and overthrow a house from its foundation, while they **teach** and transmit things **which they ought not**, that is, things that are contrary to the standard of Holy Scripture. And all this they do, not out of a desire for the salvation of people, but for their own private gain, and for the sake of **filthy lucre**, which they seek from those who are still devoted to the ceremonies of the Jews and their perverted doctrine of Justification.

One of their own prophets said, etc.) Because the Cretans were too easily swayed by these false teachers, Saint Paul criticizes their fickleness with a verse of the poet Epimenides in heroic meter: Κρῆτες ἀεὶ ψεῦσται, κακὰ θηεία, γασέρες ἀργαί, which means: "Cretans are always liars, evil beasts, lazy gluttons." Paul says that this **testimony** is **true**, because it did not come from a foreigner, to whom the manners of the Cretans might not be so well known, or from someone who harbored hatred against the nation and thus might have contrived such things against them, but from a native, who himself was a Cretan, and thus his testimony could not be easily suspected. As in other cases, domestic witnesses command little trust in praise, but in criticism, or in confessing their own faults, their testimony is most valuable, driven by the force of Truth to bear witness against themselves or those to whom they are naturally inclined, since no one is so hostile to themselves or their own people as to desire to expose domestic faults, and put themselves or their compatriots in contempt in matters that affect their family or common nation. In a single verse, the poet Epimenides notes three vices in his countrymen. First, their lightness in believing things brought from anywhere, and vanity in spreading lies. Then he criticizes their malice, being insidious and perverse men. Hence, he calls them "evil beasts." Thirdly, he points out their luxury combined with laziness in doing what is proper, thus calling them "lazy gluttons." However, he refers to the ethnic poet as a prophet, in the usual manner where poets are called seers, as if inspired by some divine force in composing their verses, in which they contemplate and attempt something above the common people, and because they often speak truths with great freedom when criticizing human vices.

Therefore, rebuke them sharply, etc.) This is an inference: Since the Cretans, according to the testimony of their own poet, are vain and frivolous, you should take this as an opportunity for vigilance, not to sleep securely, but to deter them with just severity from their ancestral frivolity, so they do not allow themselves to be swept away into error, giving heed to, and credulously believing, the **myths** and **Jewish fables**, and the **commandments** or traditions of **men who turn away from the truth**, obscuring it with their human teachings about Judaic ceremonies, as if Christians are still bound by these, about the distinction of foods, and other things that are contrary to both doctrine and Christian liberty. And because these Judaizing teachers, besides obscuring doctrine with their opinions on Justification by works, were also attacking Christian liberty, trying to uproot it with ceremonial laws from Moses, now abrogated through Christ, therefore he touches on this, declaring that **To the pure, all things are pure**, meaning that after the abolition of the distinction of foods, nothing is unclean for the pure; that is, for the faithful and those rightly taught about the use of indifferent things. Moreover, in asserting that **All things are pure to the pure**, he does not speak without qualification, as if everything, and thus even sins, are pure and permissible for the justified or pure individuals. But this general term **all things** must be understood as referring to those things that are indifferent and subject to Christian liberty. Paul presents this in such a way that while he attributes something to the pure or faithful, he denies it to the impious, faithless, and those who are unclean before God. Such were those pseudo-apostles who, due to their unbelief, had not yet been cleansed by the blood of Christ and had incorrect views about the liberty of the Gospel. About them and their likes, Paul declares that **to the impure, nothing is pure**. He calls them **defiled** and **unfaithful**. The latter epithet explains the reason for the former. They are defiled because they are faithless and lack true faith, by which alone hearts are cleansed and sprinkled with the blood of Christ, as in Acts 15. Therefore, even those things that are in themselves permissible become **unclean** for these impure ones because their **mind is defiled** by unbelief, which taints everything, just as its opposite, faith, purifies everything. Their **conscience** is also defiled, which condemns themselves and others for the use of indifferent things and dreams up sins for themselves and others where there is no sin.

They profess to know God, etc.) With this statement, Paul undermines and restrains the empty boasting of the enemies of the Gospel and Christian liberty, as if to say: "They indeed boast of their knowledge of God and claim to possess no ordinary understanding of theological matters. They pretend to have some piety towards God, but at the same time, they strongly **deny** Him **by their deeds**, like the fruits of a bad and rotten tree. While under the guise of Christianity, they fight against Christianity itself, undermine and destroy the liberty won by the blood of Christ, enslave consciences with human traditions, and ensnare the minds of the simple in the trap of error, dragging them from Christ to Satan, from truth to falsehood, from the Word of God to human traditions, hurling them into the abyss of damnation." For these actions, he calls them **detestable** to God and **abominable**, because they are **disobedient** to sound doctrine and **unfit for any good work**, being wholly preoccupied with their own petty rules and regulations, which they impose on themselves and others, neglecting true and solid piety and the works required by God's Law.

Common Places.

First. Since even in the most blessed age of the Apostles there were those who were Christians in name only, who introduced sects and taught perverse things, let us not delude ourselves into expecting a universal consensus in doctrine before the day of judgment. Rather, let us be certain that there will always be those who corrupt heavenly doctrine with their distortions and lead people away from the truth. Hence the frequent warnings about false teachers in Matthew 7, 16, 23; John 10; 1 Corinthians 11; 2

Corinthians 11; Galatians 1; Philippians 3. Especially concerning the various and horrendous deceptions of the last times, in Matthew 24; 2 Thessalonians 2; 1 Timothy 4; 1 John 2; 2 Peter 2; Revelation 12, 13, 17. "There must be heresies," says St. Paul, due to the relentless efforts of Satan, who labors with utmost diligence to continue weaving the web of deception he began, to the detriment of the Christian world. This is also partly allowed by God, both to prove those who are upright (1 Corinthians 11) and to judge those who refused to accept the beloved truth (2 Thessalonians 2).

Second. The state of the churches in Crete reminds us that the Church on earth is not entirely free from scandals and offenses. We see how diligently the devil, through false apostles, tried to spread all kinds of tares among the Cretans, to overturn the salvation of as many as possible. This is indeed his endeavor, his labor, his sole effort, as the parable in Matthew 13 teaches. Therefore, the Anabaptist faction grossly errs in rejecting the doctrine of our churches because of these scandals, and in condemning the churches themselves.

Third. The same fate of the Church should remind the watchmen and Pastors of Israel to be vigilant. From this, Paul takes the opportunity to solemnly admonish the Presbyters of the Ephesian Church not to be sluggish or secure: "Take heed to yourselves and to all the flock, in which the Holy Spirit has made you overseers, to care for the Church of God which He obtained with His own blood. For I know that after my departure fierce wolves will come in among you, not sparing the flock." (Acts 20) Again, he admonishes Titus to shut the mouths of these seducers. And this is one of the main reasons why God permits heresies to flourish: So that both Pastors and hearers may become more experienced in spiritual struggle, just as He once wanted the Israelites to be trained for war through the remaining Philistines and Canaanites in the land (Judges 3).

Fourth. Paul's grave admonition to Titus about convincing and repelling seducers is a testament to how dangerous the opinion is of those who claim that anyone can be saved in their own religion, as long as they strive for external decency of manners, give to each his due, do no wrong to anyone, and avoid outward crimes. This view errs gravely and endangers souls in two ways. Firstly, by neglecting the doctrine of faith (assuming it has no significance for salvation, however it may be composed), they place salvation in external decency of life. Secondly, this false persuasion stifles and extinguishes in themselves any effort to seek true worship of God. But if everyone could be saved in their own religion, why would there have been such careful warnings from Christ and the Apostles? They command to avoid the authors of errors as the most deadly wolves of souls, thieves, and robbers (Matthew 7, John 10, Acts 20). And why would Paul so strongly emphasize the harm done to the Cretan churches by false teachers, lamenting that entire households were overturned by them, if it were indifferent which religion one embraced?

Fifth. We have a notable testimony that in teaching, not only the truth should be presented, but also the opposing falsehood should be refuted, and, as Paul says, the mouth must be shut to those who lay traps for the flock with their perverse doctrine. Therefore, any pious zeal must be extinguished in those who either disapprove of the assertion of struggling truth or attempt to hinder it with their counsels, and who cry out that public peace is disturbed if sincere teachers vigorously oppose heretics. But God's holy will and admonition should weigh more heavily and be of greater importance to us than the clamors and unjust judgments of those truly profane in heart and mind. This is a common outcry, to which the ears of pious doctors have long been deafened. Even Christ, Stephen, Paul, and in the Old Testament, Elijah, were regarded as disturbers of public tranquility because they vigorously opposed deceivers and their corruptions. But entrusting this matter to God, they continued—despite Satan's and the world's rage—to do their duty.

Sixth. When Paul calls the pseudo-apostles "vain talkers" and "deceivers of minds," an example is set forth regarding what should be thought of those Pastors who, out of sober zeal, call heretics "wolves," "impostors," "seducers," etc. Not even this can be tolerated by profane men, and those who are more concerned with earthly peace than with God and truth, without grumbling that it is a kind of immodesty alien to Christian charity and gentleness. Although I do not deny that a certain measure should be established in this matter, yet whoever simply condemns this severity in marking the teachers and defenders of errors, must condemn the Apostle Paul himself, indeed even Christ and His servants. Has not Christ called the Jews "children of the devil," "liars"? {John 8 and 10}, and "false teachers" in general, "thieves" and "robbers"? He called his era's pseudo-doctors, the Pharisees and Scribes, hypocrites, a perverse and adulterous generation, serpents, offspring of vipers, blind and leaders of the blind, fools and blind men, whitewashed tombs. {Matthew 12 and 23.} Similarly, the Apostles call deceivers, "children of the devil," "grievous wolves," "false apostles," "ministers of Satan," "workers of iniquity," "dogs," "evil workers," "men corrupt in mind," and "reprobate concerning the faith," "impostors," "antichrists," etc. {Acts 13 and 20, 2 Corinthians 5, Philippians 3, 2 Timothy 3, 1 John 2.} Yet they have neither transgressed the bounds of modesty, nor have they been injurious to Christian love. Although in this matter, ministers of the churches will exercise prudence, so that such rebukes are directed towards edification, when the utility of the Church demands such severity. But they should not burst into other insults that harm the political reputation and fame of individuals.

Seventh. Errors in doctrine are no less deadly to men than immorality in life and manners. For through errors, the minds of men are led astray; which is why Paul calls false teachers deceivers of minds. However, the more noble the part of man which is his mind, the more dangerous is the error in doctrine than the will in life. Errors also take deeper roots in the mind than perversion of morals and thus are also more difficult to eradicate. For the dissolution of life is also argued against by reason. But an error of the mind, hiding under the guise of truth, does not endure being challenged, and it is more difficult to reach recognition of it. Therefore, let us ask God to lead us into truth by His Spirit, and by dispelling the mists of errors, give us enlightened eyes of our mind, that in His light we may see light, and never be absorbed into the deadly darkness of ignorance of God. {Ephesians 1, Psalms 13 and 36.}

Eight. In the case of false teachers converted from Judaism to Christianity who have not sincerely embraced the faith, we are given an example of how important it is to embrace not just some aspects of the true religion, but the entire, uncorrupted religion. For there is no fellowship between truth and falsehood, just as there is no communion between the light of divine knowledge and the darkness of errors. This is also why, according to Paul, even a little leaven corrupts the whole batch from the sincerity of the Gospel. Thus, the conversion of those who abandon some errors but retain others becomes useless and futile. This is similar to the ancient Samaritans (2 Kings 17) and the proselytes who transferred from paganism to Judaism under the influence of Pharisaic beliefs. Christ strongly asserts in Matthew 23 that these converts, imbued with Pharisaic opinions, become children of hell for two reasons.

Ninth. The same example teaches how difficult it is to eradicate entrenched errors. How hard was it for those from the circumcision who had turned to Christ to say goodbye to their ancestral belief in the necessity of circumcision, the distinction between foods, and other Levitical ceremonies? So much so that it took incredible effort for the Apostles to remove this deeply ingrained belief from them. This is extensively evidenced in the book of Acts and the entire Epistle to the Hebrews. How difficult was it to remove from the disciples of John the ingrained false belief that John the Baptist was the Messiah? (John 3.) How hard was it to convince the disciples of Christ that His kingdom would not be of this world? Similarly today, in the great light of the Gospel, how hard is it for people to be drawn away from their ancestral and ingrained errors, even those nearly tangible [*palpabilibus*]? This should be noted so that we do not place too much confidence in ourselves or stubbornly defend opinions refuted by God's Word, as the Papists today knowingly and willingly defend the most egregious errors with a terrible searing of their consciences.

Tenth. In well-ordered churches, care must be taken not to welcome clandestine seducers as guests. Such were those in Paul's time who overturned entire households. And such are the Anabaptists today, who go from house to house, infecting them with the poison of their fanatical opinions, or who secretly approach workers in the fields or barns during harvest, trying to entice them into their traps. To prevent these covert attempts in reformed churches, useful statutes or laws have been enacted so that such impostors are not even to be welcomed as guests, in line with the serious admonition of John, who forbids even greeting them or receiving them into homes {2 John}, since they violate the right of hospitality far more wickedly than any thieves. For they lay traps not for bodies, but for souls, and come to steal, slaughter, and destroy (John 10).

Eleventh. Again, we are reminded how destructive greed is in teachers. Motivated by this, the disruptors of the Cretan churches taught for shameful gain what they ought not to have taught. Such were also those of whom Paul writes in 2 Corinthians 2: "We are not like many, peddling the Word of God"; that is, adapting their teachings to please people for the sake of profit. And they are not good shepherds of the sheep, but hirelings, who think that godliness is a means to financial gain (1 Timothy 6). When greed prevailed in the Papacy, it caused the entire matter of Religion to be turned into the most disgraceful trade and business of the great harlot of Babylon. {Revelation 18} Just as Peter had foretold, there would come in the last days false teachers, who through greed would exploit us with fabricated stories. {2 Peter 2} However, the minister of God should heed Paul's admonition: "Withdraw from such people. For great gain is godliness with contentment," etc. (1 Timothy 6).

Twelfth. It often happens that certain vices are familiar to certain nations. Just as fickleness was familiar to the Cretans, today Italians are known for licentiousness, Germans for drunkenness, Turks, Tartars, and other peoples who are farther from cultured humanity, for cruelty and barbarity; and other nations have other vices and sins. However, we should not be swayed by the multitude of people in approving or following sins, even if entire populations contaminate themselves with them. For the multitude of sinners does not provide a defense for impiety, and the wrath of God devours both individual sinners and the dense masses of many. Therefore, the Holy Spirit so earnestly warns us not to follow the multitude in sinning, nor to allow ourselves to be bound with the cords of iniquity with the wicked, nor to yoke ourselves in ungodliness with them (Exodus 23, Isaiah 5, Sirach 7, 2 Corinthians 6).

Thirteenth. That the Cretans, previously infamous for their vanity, were not disdained by the Lord to be called to the recognition of His Son, is a clear testimony of His goodness and philanthropy [φιλανθρωπίας], which shone on the nations without any regard for their own worthiness. This is also the reason why the Apostles so often remind the Gentiles of what they once were, so that they might more deeply contemplate God's philanthropy and learn to proclaim more fervently the virtues of Him who called them gratuitously without works, from darkness into His marvelous light, as is evident in the sermons found in Romans 6 and 13; 1 Corinthians 6 and 12; Ephesians 2; 1 Peter 1, 2, and 4.

Fourteenth. We have a very clear testimony that it is permissible to devote some part of study to the reading of secular authors, provided that it is done with judgment and discretion, distinguishing the good things found in them from the bad. Paul was excellently versed in the reading of secular writers, even of Gentile poets. He quotes a heroic verse from Epimenides: "Cretans are always liars, evil beasts, lazy gluttons." From Aratus in Acts 17: "For we are also His offspring." From Menander: "Evil communications corrupt good manners" (Corinthians 15). {*Iambic Senarius.*} This is to be noted against the intemperance of the Anabaptists, who completely disapprove of reading the works of Gentiles and condemn Christian schools on the grounds that books of the Gentiles are read to the studious youth. This audacity is rebuffed by the example of the Apostle, whom we see not only read poets but also was able to aptly cite them as the occasion demanded.

Fifteenth. However, it should not be approved that some preachers, due to a certain misplaced zeal, misuse Paul's example by quoting entire Greek or Latin sentences from secular authors in front of the congregation, more to show off their extensive reading than for any benefit that might accrue to the listener. Indeed, outside of sermons, when we write or speak, the use of such quotations can be quite significant. But in popular sermons, quoting Greek or Latin sentences to those who do not understand these languages is considered inappropriate by the Apostle himself (1 Corinthians 14). Nor should they frequently use them translated into German in their sermons. Paul did this for a specific reason: To reprove and convince those who were either pagans (such as the Athenians in Acts 17) or had only recently converted from paganism, using the testimony of their own poets. The situation of our people is different, as anyone can understand. Sometimes, however, it may not be inappropriate to quote examples or sayings of the Gentiles, but this should be done very sparingly, and almost only by way of comparison, when it is taught in application that even the nations themselves, led solely by the light of reason, recognized the need to avoid this or that vice and to pursue this or that virtue: how much more should we observe this distinction between honorable and dishonorable, who, in addition to the light of nature, have the voice of divine Word, which teaches what God wants us to do and what not to do.

Sixteenth. Heavenly doctrine should not be contaminated with human fables or even the precepts and traditions of men. Just as a new patch does not fit an old garment, which would result in a worse tear, according to Christ {Matthew 9}, and just as chaff has nothing to do with wheat, so too the Word of God has no business with the precepts of men, by which God is vainly worshiped. {Jeremiah 23} "Every plantation which My Heavenly Father has not planted will be uprooted." {Matthew 15} Therefore, the Lord strictly commanded His people not to do anything according to their own judgment in matters of worship, but entirely according to the directive of the Word (Deuteronomy 4 and 12). When the Papists neglected this Rule and replaced it with the contrary "Rule of Good Intentions," as they called it, it resulted in an immense accumulation of human traditions, and the precepts of men reigned in all chairs and pulpits instead of the doctrine of Christ, the Prophets, and the Apostles. Even the most insipid fables, no better than those Jewish ones, devised by idle monks, suppressed and exiled the teaching of Christ, the Prophets, and the Apostles.

Seventeenth. The Apostle's rule ("All things are pure for the pure") reminds us of Christian liberty under Christ's Kingdom. Indeed, before Christ's coming, the Fathers lived under the pedagogue of numerous Levitical ceremonies; they could easily be rendered unclean according to the law, hence the need for many washings. But under the New Testament, all things are clean for the clean (as it pertains to external and indifferent things), and even those things forbidden to the Israelite people are now allowed. For the ceremonial law, based in decrees, has been abrogated, and we have been set free through Christ. Thus, nothing that enters the mouth defiles a person, as Christ Himself has judged (Matthew 15). The Apostle concurs with this saying, writing: "If you have died with Christ from the elements of the world, why, as if you were still living in the world, do you submit to decrees? Do not handle, do not taste, do not touch, all of which perish with use, according to the commandments and teachings of men" (Colossians 2). This hypocrisy in the Papacy nearly extinguished the Christian faith entirely. However, we should stand in the liberty with which Christ has set us free, and not allow ourselves to be entangled again with a yoke of bondage. We have been called to liberty, only do not use liberty as an opportunity for the flesh (Galatians 5).

Eighteenth. The same rule, by which all things are declared pure for the pure, clearly teaches that as soon as the idolatrous abuse of the Pontifical Mass is removed, the altar on which the mass was formerly celebrated is no longer impure, but falls among *adiaphora* (indifferent things) and is subject to Christian liberty. It has been purified by the Word of God, which loudly declares that ALL

82

things are clean for the pure. As this Apostolic statement is echoed in different words in Romans 14, where Paul argues: For I know and am persuaded by the Lord Jesus, that NOTHING is unclean in itself, except to the one who considers something to be unclean: to him it is unclean. And since the vessels of the Temple, once carried into the temple of the idol in Babylon by King Nebuchadnezzar and dreadfully profaned by the profane and Cyclopean banquet of King Belshazzar, when later restored to the Jews by Cyrus, could again be used in the performance of sacred worship with a clear conscience, despite the fact that at that time everything had to be most meticulously clean according to the law, how much more under the liberty of the New Testament can altars, chalices, and other items once used for the abuse of the Pontifical Mass, with abuses removed, be used without sin for the performance of true worship? For they are not unclean in themselves before God, whose creatures they remain, and are therefore pure. For the earth is the Lord's, and its fullness. Paul teaches this to be so true that he explicitly allows eating of things offered to idols, or (as he himself explains) to demons, in 1 Corinthians 10, provided that the one who eats does so with an unhesitating conscience and does not give offense to the weak.

Nineteenth. We are warned about the nature of unbelief, which pollutes everything in a man. It contaminates his mind and conscience, as the Apostle says here. [It contaminates] his person: because it is impossible for a man to please God without faith (Hebrews 11). [It contaminates] his works: because whatever is not of faith is sin (Romans 14). It corrupts all worship and renders it useless (Isaiah 1). It even turns a man's prayer into sin (Psalm 109). Therefore, let us ask God to purify our hearts through the faith of Jesus Christ, and thus our works, commended by faith, will be pleasing to Him.

Twentieth. Hypocrisy, which imitates piety, markets itself under the attractive label of piety, and splendidly simulates piety, while in reality it denies it through its actions. Today, many boast greatly about God and their knowledge of Him and maintain an appearance of godliness, as Paul says in 2 Timothy 3, but they have denied its power: They draw near to God with their lips, but their hearts are far from Him (Isaiah 29). All their boasting is like a tinkling cymbal and a resounding brass (1 Corinthians 13), like springs without water, like clouds carried by a storm, for whom the blackness of darkness is reserved forever. (2 Peter 2) "Not everyone who says, 'Lord, Lord,' will enter the kingdom of heaven, but only he who does the will of My Father who is in heaven." (Matthew 7)

Chapter Two.

Argument.

Paul instructs Titus on how he should individually admonish every Christian regarding their duties. Then he adds a general reason derived from the appearance of God's saving grace, which should inspire all people to pursue piety.

FIRST PART.

But speak thou the things which become sound doctrine.) The beginning of this chapter is connected through contrast with the end of the preceding one. For, as opposed to the trifles, fables, and human precepts with which the false-apostles were fruitlessly occupied, as he had described, Paul contrasts necessary doctrine and salutary exhortation to the people. It is as if he says: "You, my dear Titus, do not burden the Church entrusted to your care with those vain commentaries, by which men are taught no aspect of piety. But **speak** those things **which become sound doctrine**, so that your sermons may be drawn from the clearest sources of Israel, and each point confirmed by suitable testimonies from the Sacred Scriptures. Also, let the exhortations be fitting and conform to sound doctrine, so that they may offer some edification to the listeners." And this is the general command, which the Apostle now, by a certain distribution, scatters among different ages and classes of people, prescribing for each their own exhortations (παραινέσεις) according to which they should perform their duties. And first, he shows which virtues are primarily to be encouraged in the elderly.

Elders to be sober) the first virtue is sobriety, which is especially necessary for elders, both because their almost natural dryness makes them crave wine, to restore their failing radical moisture like a kindling and sustenance, and because of the weakness of their bodies, even moderately consumed wine quickly overwhelms and intoxicates them. Once intoxicated, they easily say and do things that debase their authority and offend the young. Therefore, he especially wants them to strive for sobriety, as old age is more easily lulled by wine.

Grave) The second virtue, particularly adorning old age, is σεμνότης, gravity in speech, manners, and in the overall demeanor of body and mind. They should not be frivolous, either in highlighting things that are unseemly, or in recounting those matters by which the tender youth may be offended.

Healthy in faith) This is the third requirement, calling for them to both hold firm to sound doctrine themselves and to brightly set a good example for the youth in faithfully embracing the same.

Charity) Just as he demands orthodox faith, so, too, does the Apostle require sincere charity from the elderly. Also, **patience** to endure the discomforts of old age with equanimity, so they are not led to impious murmuring against God, which would be contrary to and hostile towards faith; nor to bitterness of spirit against their neighbor, which would harm charity. And that is the guidance for older men. From here, he now transitions to elderly women, advising Titus on what acts of piety and humanity they should be encouraged to undertake.

First, **that they be in apparel which becometh holiness**) as if to say: It is fitting for an elderly woman to be religious, whom nature itself, almost reaching its end, should draw away from the desires of this world, so that, satiated with this life, they may wholly devote themselves to the Word and religious piety, and prepare for a blissful departure from this corrupt world. Therefore, their spirit should be adorned with religion, and their body with attire that not only suits religion but also befits their age. Elderly women should not emulate the adornment of younger women, but according to their age, they should wear respectable clothing.

Not slanderers) who, out of the irritability that old age often brings among its other evils, burst into slander and accusations.

Not given to much wine) Although it is permissible for them to use a little wine to restore their vital fluids, the Apostle does not want them to be addicted to wine, lest they begin to act foolishly because of it.

Teach what is good) Blessed Paul wants older matrons to not only conduct themselves honorably in every respect but also to **teach** young women. What should they teach? **What is honorable**, he says, meaning what is appropriate both for civil and Christian moral decency. This general statement is further clarified by a specific enumeration of duties that old women should teach young women. First, "**to make young women modest**") In Greek, the word is σωφρονίζειν, which commends modesty coupled with prudence in their words and deeds. This somewhat general statement is now dispersed into specifics. First, he says: **to love their husbands**) that is, to cherish their husbands with sincere love and conjugal affection. Next, **to love their children**) This is also not the least thing that old women should teach young women, to love their children, not with that blind affection where many mothers indulge their children in everything, but with true and genuine love, wishing them eternal well-being, and thus sanctifying them in the fear of God and religion. **To be sober-minded**) Older women should teach young women to be temperate, so that nothing is done improperly out of luxury of spirit. Similarly, **pure**, ἁγναὶ, chaste, keeping the faith given to their husbands, not transferring the love owed solely to their husbands elsewhere, or giving in to unpermitted desires. **Workers at home,** οἰκοθροὶ, who do not wander elsewhere idly, neglecting the care of household affairs, but who keep themselves within their homes and manage household tasks well, so that the family does not suffer any loss. **Kind)** or benevolent, gentle, and charitable. **Submissive to their own husbands)** obedient to their husbands in all things that do not harm piety. To this admonition, St. Paul adds this most serious reason: **so that the Word of God may not be reviled**, which tends to happen when women professing religion debase it with vices and expose it to the mockery of unbelieving men.

Young men) After speaking of three distinct groups of people differentiated by age, namely older men, elder women, and younger women, he now turns to young men: **Urge them,** he says, **to be** σωφρονίζειν **sober-minded.** By this term, he requires not only sobriety as opposed to drunkenness, but also encompasses σωφροσύνη, the preserver of all virtues and expeller of opposing vices, or sober prudence, to act rightly, moderately, and according to piety and virtue, so that nothing contradictory to Christian prudence and moderation is committed. He adds, **In everything set them an example by doing what is good.)** Here, he shifts the conversation from the young men to Titus himself, in this sense: "I wish you, O Titus, to exhort others in such a way that you not only arouse them to duties of piety with words, but also instruct them with your example, with holy life and conduct: **showing yourself to be a pattern of good works**, like a polished mirror, in which they looking upon it, may have a model to shape and adorn their own lives, and follow your exhortations more eagerly if they understand that they are validated by the example of your holy conduct. **In your teaching show integrity**, or incorruptibility; that is, present yourself as an example of doctrinal sincerity, free from all corruptions. In behavior, demonstrate σεμνότητα, **gravity and decency.** And in your speeches, whether for teaching or exhortation, let there be **sound speech that cannot be condemned. So that those who oppose you may be ashamed because they have nothing bad to say about us.**") He adds the reason why Titus should strive for the highest standards of true piety in everything; namely, to shut the mouths of slanderers with his blameless life when they find nothing they can justly criticize, no matter how focused they are on finding any opportunity to slander.

Urge the slaves, etc.) He descends to the lowest status, that of the slaves. In the times of the Apostles, slaves were bondmen, with their masters having power over their life and death. Lest the slaves under the pretext of the Gospel and the promised spiritual freedom attempt to shake off the yoke of physical servitude, or at least perform their duties with less diligence, he instructs Titus to remind even these of their responsibilities. First, **to be obedient to their own masters**, and **to please them**, or to conform themselves **in all things** that can be performed with a good conscience by Christian men. **Not answering back**) He addresses common vices of slaves, who often grumble when reprimanded or punished for neglecting their duties, something Paul wants to be foreign to Christian slaves. **Not pilfering**) This is also a prevalent issue among slaves, either secretly stealing from their masters or handling their possessions so unfaithfully that their value decreases rather than increases. **But showing all good fidelity, etc.**) He demands a virtue contrary to the listed vices, and their remedy from the slaves, **faith** or fidelity, and that **good** kind, by which they solely promote the welfare of their masters to the best of their ability, and avoid any harm in all ways. **So that they may adorn the doctrine of God our Savior in all things**) An effective reason is given for faithfulness to be shown by Christian slaves: Because by their fidelity and obedience, they will adorn the doctrine of the eternal God, and our

Savior, the Lord Jesus Christ, so that even unbelievers may have a reason to recognize it, or be deprived of any opportunity to slander.

Common Places.

First. The epithet by which the Apostle Paul proclaims the heavenly doctrine with the name of health reminds us of the power and efficacy of the Word of God. It revives a person languishing in sins, indeed, resurrects one dead in sins, as if by the living and incorruptible seed of God, and makes him healthy, strong, and vigorous for every good work. {Eph. 2, 1 Pet. 2} It refreshes the soul of a person fainting in the heat of temptations (Psa. 119). It gladdens the heart, enlightens the eyes, and is altogether a most present remedy and antidote for driving away the diseases of the soul. Like that saving salt Christ mentioned, it also preserves the whole person from putrefaction and perpetual corruption. Therefore, it is rightly called HEALTHY Doctrine. False doctrine, however, is sickly, infecting a person with lethal poison, and spreading like gangrene until it consumes as many as possible, and absorbs them into eternal death. Hence, Pastors should speak healthy doctrine, not sickly. They should also shape their exhortations so that they conform to healthy doctrine and are entirely constructed from it, just as the Apostle admonishes his Titus in this place.

Second. Ministers of the churches should not only institute general admonitions for cultivating piety, but also recognize that among Christians there are different ranks and orders, and distinct duties within them. Therefore, they should be well-prepared to appropriately exhort individuals of any condition and age as the situation requires. This approach was followed by Paul in 1 Corinthians 11; Ephesians 5 and 6; Colossians 3 and 4, as well as by Peter in his first Epistle, chapters 2 and 3; and by John in his first Canonical letter, chapter 2.

Third. Let the elderly never forget what this faithful servant and Apostle of Christ requires of them. Indeed, old age is venerable, as God Himself has decreed and commanded it to be honored by law. {Leviticus 19} But truly venerable are those elders who, along with their years and gray hair, have combined Christian prudence, wisdom, and gravity, which is the crown of the aged walking in the path of righteousness (Proverbs 16 and Sirach 25). On the contrary, those who, along with their age and years, have grown in malice and impiety (as is often found, who shamelessly recount their past crimes before the youth, or indulge in drunkenness or other sins), what should be thought of them is not concealed by the Holy Spirit, as stated in Isaiah 65 and Sirach 25.

Fourth. But elderly women must also diligently observe the text prescribed to them. Paul's admonition is very necessary because of the unrestrained wickedness of some, who, taught in the school of impiety, know almost nothing but to slander and spread rumors, either heard from anywhere or fabricated out of malice, to set people against each other and disturb their peace. There are also not a few who incite younger women to disobedience towards their husbands or are a source of levity for others. This leads to many secret marriages among the young being contracted without the legitimate consent of parents, and many other actions alien to all piety being planned, which Satan accomplishes through impious old women as convenient instruments. Elderly women who want to prove themselves to God and sensible people should encourage young women according to Paul's instructions towards every duty of piety; and they themselves should also be adorned with upright morals and be religious, serving God with fasts and prayers, day and night, as we read about the prophetess Hannah in Luke 2.

Fifth. An ideal of a pious and honorable matron is presented, as Paul wants a wife to love her husband, love her children, be sober, pure, a homemaker, gentle and kind, and submissive to her husband. This exquisite image beautifully aligns with other descriptions by the Holy Spirit of wise and virtuous women. Regarding love for husbands, Lamuel teaches this in Proverbs 31, where, depicting a good woman through the brush of the Holy Spirit, he desires her to be so devoted to her husband that he can safely and confidently trust in her. Sirach says that she should treat her husband well, cheer his heart, and make life peaceful. As for loving children, Nature itself sanctifies this, so much so that if any woman neglects them, she is rightly considered to have denied the faith and to be worse than an unbeliever (1 Timothy 5). Solomon testifies to the honor of a woman being σώφρων, wise, proclaiming a prudent woman as a gift from God, incomparable to anything in human affairs, in Proverbs 12, 19, and 31. The purity or chastity required in Paul's ideal is also praised by Sirach, who writes in chapter 26 that nothing is more precious than this, while elsewhere, a beautiful woman lacking in the virtue of Chastity is compared to a pig adorned with a golden necklace (Proverbs 11). That a Christian woman should be a homemaker, οἰκουρὸν, aligns precisely with Psalm 128, where she is compared to a vine clinging to the walls of her house, adhering to it and not departing. The Holy Spirit did not hesitate to extensively celebrate this domestic care and household labor of a wise woman in Proverbs 31. Wisdom, along with Apostle Paul, also praises her kindness in Proverbs 31 by Lamuel, illustrating how she provides necessary food for her household and extends generous hands to relieve the need of the poor. Finally, the submission owed to husbands, briefly touched upon by Paul here, is more extensively commended elsewhere, with the prominent example of the Church, which submits herself in every respect to her Spouse, so that women may learn to obey their husbands. For more on this, see Ephesians 5 and 1 Peter 3.

Sixth. There is a memorable saying, to be perpetually remembered by each and every Pastor, in which Paul admonishes Titus to present himself in every way as a model of good works in teaching and in conduct. Such Pastors build up twice as much. Others, who teach well but live poorly, undermine with one hand what they build with the other, and all their exhortations lose their authority because the Pastor's life diverges from them in every way. More about this was said in the first chapter.

Seventh. But this also is to be observed by all Christians, which Paul specifically impresses here on Titus, and then on servants, teaching that among other reasons, sanctity must be pursued in order to cut off the opportunity for slander, and to adorn the teaching of our Savior God. This reasoning is vehemently pressed by the Prophets and Apostles. Nathan reproaches David for causing the nations to blaspheme God's name through his sins. {2 Sam. 12} The same complaint is made tragically by Isaiah and Ezekiel about the people of Judah, and in the New Testament by Paul. {Isa. 52, Eze. 36, Rom. 2} Indeed, the course of the Gospel is not lightly hindered when the teaching is disfigured by the sins of those who profess to be its adherents. Therefore, let us strive with all our might to adorn the profession of the doctrine with the sanctity of life and to shut the mouths of slanderers. "Conduct yourselves honorably among the Gentiles," says Peter, "so that, though they slander you as evildoers, they may see your good deeds and glorify God on the day he visits us" (1 Peter 2). And he says that even unbelieving husbands may be won over by the holy conduct of their wives, even without words (1 Peter 3).

Eighth. Paul, in earnestly commending doctrinal purity to his Titus, clearly teaches how important it is for Pastors of the Church to be sincere in doctrine. For their error is deadly to the churches, drawing the flock of hearers into the fellowship of destruction. Indeed, the word of the Savior is most true, "If the blind lead the blind, both will fall into a pit" (Luke 6). This is also openly declared by Isaiah about the teachers of his time, in chapter 9. Therefore, it is a not insignificant temptation of the devil when the simple and common people, beguiled by the external appearance of sanctity of the Anabaptists, immediately join themselves to them, not caring about the soundness of their doctrine. However, the churches are well provided for if they have teachers who are orthodox in doctrine and of exemplary conduct in life. As the Church, praying in its solemn Litany for the ministers of the Word, sings and prays that they may be preserved in the saving word and a holy life.

Ninth. On the duty of servants and maidservants. It consists in obedience and fidelity, that they serve their masters with fear and trembling, in simplicity of heart as unto Christ, not with eyeservice as men pleasers, {Ephesians 6} but as servants of Christ, knowing that they will receive the reward of the inheritance from the Lord. {Colossians 3} For he who is faithful in a little will be put in charge of much (Matthew 25). Therefore, let servants and maidservants observe the will of their masters and mistresses (Psalm 123), show themselves compliant, and demonstrate complete good faith in advancing their masters' interests, doing whatever can be done without compromising their piety, so that in these ways they may adorn the teaching of our Savior. But if something is commanded that is contrary to the Word of God, they should remember the rule: "We ought to obey God rather than men" (Acts 5). Just as Joseph refused to comply with his mistress's indecent request (Genesis 39).

Tenth. The fact that even servants in their servile condition are said to adorn the teaching of God our Savior is an argument that they are not in a worse position before God because of their lowly status. For in Christ Jesus, there is neither slave nor free (Galatians 3). And those who are slaves according to the flesh can be free in the Lord (1 Corinthians 7), since they, too, have been redeemed by the blood of Christ, with whom there is no partiality. Hence Job fears to do wrong even to the least servant, mindful that he, too, is created by the Lord (Job 31). These words are spoken for the consolation of such miserable and lowly persons, whom the Lord loves, provided they believe in Christ and carry out their duties with faithfulness and diligence.

Eleventh. Finally, we should note the testimony of the divinity of Christ in Paul's words: "to adorn the teaching of our Savior, GOD." It is well known to all Christians who this Savior is; namely, our Lord Jesus Christ, besides whom there is no other salvation or Savior (Acts 4). He is openly called God here—indeed, the same God who in Isaiah 43 proclaims: "I, even I, am Jehovah, and apart from me there is no SAVIOR."

SECOND PART.

After the previous admonitions, through which Saint Paul addressed the Christian life individually according to different ages and conditions, now connects a certain general, yet powerfully effective, reason. This is derived from the beneficial appearance of divine grace, which ought to instruct and encourage all people—regardless of their sex, age, and condition—to turn away from the perverse desires of worldly passions and to cultivate a life of holiness and the practice of good works.

The grace of God that brings salvation has appeared to all men, etc.) This is a brief but exceedingly forceful, brilliant, and very befitting exhortation of such a great Apostle, reminding

Christians of the inestimable gift of God, who has allowed a new and welcome Light to shine for those sitting in the eternal darkness of death, dispelling the deadly and fatal shadows into which all were engulfed. And what is that Light? It is the **grace** of God, which, turning away His face full of wrath due to sins, now allows His most serene face of grace to shine. And indeed, not without great fruit, for he calls that grace of God **salvific**, as if it were the primary source and fountain of eternal salvation. To whom has this grace of God appeared? To **ALL** men, excluding none, nor excluding anyone through some absolute decree of God. Has it appeared, then, so that relying on this philanthropy of God, we may afterwards wantonly indulge? Not at all; but, rather, with the opposite purpose. For it **teaches us** like a kind of Pedagogue, **that, denying ungodliness, etc.** He means to say, "The grace of God is for us a guide and teacher towards sanctity of life, instructing and prescribing what henceforth we should abandon and what we should pursue. It commands us to **deny ungodliness**, idolatry, and all sorts of vices; it commands us to avoid **worldly desires**, which the world or depraved flesh craves." Here the Apostle's emphatic word is to be noted, wanting all these things to be **denied**, that is, to bid farewell to them and renounce them, as with those things Christians should rather wage war than ever return to their vomit.

 Soberely, righteously, and godly we should live, etc.) This is the second thing to which the dawning mercy of God provokes us; namely, to lead a holy life, which he expressed with these three terms: soberly, righteously, and godly. With the term **soberly**, he advises us to handle all things in moderation and with prudence regarding ourselves. The second term (**righteously**) shapes our life as it should be towards our neighbor; namely just, trying not to commit any injustice or inflict unjust force upon them. The term **godly** demands faith towards God, hope, invocation, and fear of Him. Within this scope of virtues, like a circle of Christian perfection, he wants our lives to rotate and revolve.

In the present world) St. Paul reminds us that the pursuit of piety should begin in this world and be completed in the next. He also shows the remedy to revive those who are faltering in the race of piety, by setting forth the magnificent reward that will be attained at the Coming of the Lord Jesus Christ for those who have earnestly continued that commendable course, concerning which he preaches: **Looking for that blessed, etc.**) He wants the faithful to be motivated by the expectation of promised goods, so they do not grow lethargic in the arena of Christian piety and innocence, but instead strive with unceasing effort toward the goal set before them, spurred on by the **hope** of that truly **blessed** promise made in His Word by Him who cannot lie or deceive. He links this hope with the **expectation** of Christ's Coming because only then will the things hoped for be revealed and given to the faithful to possess fully. He refers to Christ's Coming in common parlance as **appearance**, because He who is now invisibly present at God's right hand and moves among us, will then appear visibly, coming in the clouds of heaven. But he describes this ἐπιφάνεια or **appearance** of Christ with a remarkable notation, for he speaks of the appearance of **Glory**, making a kind of antithesis between the second coming and the first, in that Christ first appeared in the form of a Servant, but in His second Coming, He will appear in glory—not simply glory, but in the glory of the Father, as He clearly professes elsewhere. Moreover, Christ Himself, who will appear in this glorious coming, he calls **God**, and indeed **the great God**, indicating with a notable epithet that the name of God is attributed to Christ not as to Angels or Magistrates (because of the Majesty of their office), but in its proper sense because of His eternal Deity, as the true and great God, greater than any other. But he also calls Him **Savior**, referring to the office He undertook on earth, saving or delivering His faithful people from all sins. For this reason, He was also called **Jesus**, as the Angel interprets, in Mat. 1. And also **Christ**, since He was anointed to this sublime office with the fullness of the Spirit and Power beyond all measure. He soon adds an explanation of this office, along with a designation of the goal congruent with the exhortation he has set forth. It also contains an argument of utmost effectiveness for sanctifying the pursuit of piety, as he recalls the precious ransom with which we have been liberated from sins, namely that JESUS CHRIST, the great God, **gave Himself for us** into the most ignominious death on the cross. Therefore, since Christ has freed us from the tyranny of sin into freedom at such a precious cost, why would we voluntarily plunge ourselves again into the filth of ungodliness? Rather, the Apostle wants to say, Christ gave Himself for us with the purpose **to redeem us from all iniquity**, which conflicts with God's Law, simultaneously magnifying the greatness of Christ's benefit, proclaiming that we are redeemed and freed from **all** iniquity through the most holy redemption of Christ. **And to purify unto Himself a peculiar people, etc.**) The goal related to the previous one, except it implies an antithesis between iniquity, from which Christ redeems us, and the pursuit of good works, for which that redemption designates us. Therefore, he says that Christ gave Himself for us **to purify** us with His blood **unto Himself as a peculiar people**, that is, to select us as His special possession, as those who are no longer their own, but have come under His service by the price of His blood, so that we are wholly devoted to Him alone, worship, revere, and exclusively serve Him. **Zealous of good works**) He expresses the manner in which we should serve Him, who claims us as His own by the right of redemption; namely, through the pursuit of **good works**, not those concocted by human reason, but those which God requires in His holy Law. The Christian people are emphatically called ζηλωτὴν καλῶν ἔργων, that is, zealous for good works, fervently pursuing good deeds and directing all their efforts to prove themselves in holy services to God and their Redeemer Christ. **Speak these things**) He repeats the proposition of the second chapter. Just as he had said at the beginning of the chapter, **"But you, speak the things which are proper for sound doctrine,"** after having enumerated these specifics and illuminated them with a general reason, he now repeats the same proposition, as if to say: **"These are the things I want you to speak and exhort,** and these are the weights of the reasons by which you can strike the souls of your listeners, so that they may comply with your holy admonitions. Conversely, **rebuke** sternly those things that are contrary to the rules for instituting a Christian life that have just been given. And do this part of your duty **with all authority**, not lukewarmly, but with pious and fervent zeal. **Let no man despise you** for thus urging them to works of piety, or laugh off your admonitions as if they were thunderbolts out of the mud. You should also institute them in such a way, so confirm them with the testimonies of the Holy Spirit, and present them with such gravity, as if they were born not on the tongue, but in the heart, so that no one may have any occasion either to despise you or to scoff at your salutary admonitions."

Common Places.

First. Concerning the ineffable mercy of God, which has shone upon, and appeared to, the human race through the saving incarnation and advent of our Lord Jesus Christ. This mercy is exceedingly magnified when compared to our extreme misery. For we, walking in the formidable region of the shadow of death, indeed clinging in the jaws of the devil and hell, and on the brink of eternal perdition, God called us from death to life, from the darkness of perpetual misery to the desired light of blessedness, from destruction to salvation; and this, not because of our merit, but solely by His saving grace, through the tender mercy of our God, by which the Day-spring from on high has visited us, to give light to those who sit in darkness and the shadow of death, to guide our feet into the way of peace. {Luke 1} The most certain pledge of His love He gave us, His only begotten Son, that whoever believes in Him should not perish but have eternal life. {John 3} For this indescribable gift, let us sing and give eternal thanks to His goodness.

Second. Since the Apostle derives arguments from the free mercy of God, which justifies us without any merit of our own, to persuade Christians to cultivate religious piety and holiness, it becomes clear that the foul accusation of the Papists, alleging that preaching about grace hinders the course of piety and weakens the zeal for doing good, is baseless. What arguments could be more weighty or more effective in inciting the zeal for good works and strengthening new obedience than those that the blessed Apostle has either explicitly drawn from the article of free salvation of men or left Christians to contemplate? For instance: The grace of God has shone for this purpose, that being rescued from the kingdom of darkness, you may live eternally. Why, then, would you willingly plunge yourself back into the former darkness of misery through impenitence? Also: The Grace of God instructs us to live soberly, justly, and chastely: Therefore, such a salutary Teacher must be heeded. Similarly: Christ gave Himself for us, that He might redeem us from all iniquity: Why, then, should we, through a miserable pursuit of sinning, again enslave ourselves to iniquity, from which we have been freed by such a precious ransom (λύτρον)? Namely, not with corruptible gold or silver, but with the precious blood of Christ, as of a lamb without blemish and without spot. {1 Peter 1} And again: He redeemed us to be His own possession. Therefore, we are no longer our own to sin as we please, but we must serve Christ. As Paul also teaches elsewhere: "You are not your own; for you have been bought with a price" (1 Cor. 6). Furthermore: "He gave Himself for us, that He might purify us and choose us as a people zealous for good works, a chosen generation, a royal priesthood, a people who have become His own." {1 Peter 2.} Therefore, to profane such a holy calling with sins against conscience, how vile, how abominable would that be? Are these not compelling reasons to sanctify piety? Reflecting on these, David expressly sings: "With You is abundant redemption, THAT YOU MAY BE FEARED": indeed teaching that free forgiveness of sins is an incentive to reverence for the Divine. {Psalm 130} But since the opportunity to speak on this doctrine will present itself in the third chapter, I deliberately forego a more extensive explanation now.

Third. The significant and noteworthy statement of Paul that the saving grace of God has appeared to ALL MEN is of utmost importance for everyone to observe. From this, we can undeniably conclude that those who write of some being rejected and condemned to inevitable damnation by an absolute decree of God from all eternity, clearly deviate from the doctrine of the Apostle Paul.[1] Setting aside for now the testimonies of other Prophets and Apostles, he [Paul] makes no distinction of any person from this saving grace of God, except through their own disbelief and impenitence. In Romans 11, Paul proclaims with the clearest voice that God has consigned all to disobedience, that He may have mercy on all. And in his writing to Timothy, he states: "God desires ALL MEN to be saved and to come to the knowledge of the truth." {1 Timothy 2} For there is one God, and one mediator between God and men, Jesus Christ, who gave Himself as a ransom for ALL. Therefore, Christ is again said to be the Savior of ALL MEN, especially of those who believe. {1 Timothy 4} This statement effectively overturns the gloss of the proponents of absolute decree, who interpret

---

1 Hunnius is addressing the views of the Calvinists.

these universal promises as applying only to those whom they arbitrarily deem as the elect. The very clause (especially of believers) makes it even clearer that by "all men" in the preceding words, he does not mean believers alone (since he distinctly differentiates them from others), but encompasses all human beings. Christ is the Savior of all these, because He died for all (1 John 2), even for the reprobate, who perish and are condemned through their own fault, as it is written: "They deny the Lord who bought them, bringing upon themselves swift destruction" (2 Peter 2).

Fourth. The Apostle's text reminds us of the promise made in our vow in Baptism. In Baptism, God's salvific grace shone upon us, transforming us from being by nature children of wrath into children and heirs of eternal bliss. In return, we solemnly pledged obedience to God, renouncing Satan and his works, and denying ungodliness along with worldly lusts. Therefore, we should remember our vow and not sacrilegiously break away from what we have solemnly committed to. If we have fallen away due to the devil's deceit through reigning sins, let us not persist in our fall, but rather (as Jeremiah 8 advises), through repentance, be restored [in our Baptism] with God, which remains unchangeable on His part, so that as soon as we earnestly recover from the snares of impiety (which depends on the power of God, who should not be tempted against conscience by sins), He may accept us back into the embrace of His grace under the originally initiated covenant. {2 Timothy 2} For if we are faithless, He remains faithful, for He cannot deny Himself: provided we renew our vow with a firm resolution to henceforth abstain from carnal desires, which war against the soul, as Peter states. {1 Peter 2}

Fifth. The Apostle Paul teaches that the world is placed under the evil one, when he suggests that its desires are so arranged that Christians must flee them with all effort. Therefore, John also writes: "He who loves the world does not have the love of the Father in him." {1 John 2} For what is in the world, such as the lust of the flesh, the lust of the eyes, and the pride of life, are not from the Father. And James, agreeing with this, says: "Adulterers and adulteresses, do you not know that friendship with the world is enmity with God?" {James 4} Therefore, whoever wishes to be a friend of the world becomes an enemy of God. Therefore, let us conduct ourselves as foreigners in the world, withdrawing our minds from those things that are in the world, and with hearts lifted up to God, let us seek the things above, not earthly things. {Colossians 3} For the world passes away with its desires, but he who does the will of God remains forever (1 John 2).

Sixth. Let each person regard this circle of the entire Christian life as entrusted to them, so that in all their words and deeds they live soberly and moderately with respect to themselves, justly towards their neighbor, and piously towards God. Thus the circle will be completed, within whose bounds all measures of right and decency are contained. For he who lives intemperately and imprudently in his affairs injures himself. He who does not live justly harms the love of his neighbor. And finally, he who does not live piously strikes at the Majesty of God with his impiety. Therefore, let us give to ourselves, our neighbor, and to God what is their due. In this way, we will be acceptable to God and approved by men.

Seventh. The pursuit of piety should not be postponed until the final stretch of our life, but in the present age, not only should its beginnings be made, but also progress. For he who does not live soberly, justly, and piously in this present life will come too late, like the foolish virgins, who, having not prepared their lamps in time, hear the doors closed and the words: "I do not know you" (Matthew 25). Therefore, let us not delay in turning to the Lord, and in living piously and holily in His sight (Isaiah 55, Sirach 5).

Eighth. The blessed hope mentioned by the Apostle should inspire and strengthen us in the race of faith and piety, as if competing in the stadium for the longed-for possession of promised things. Indeed, if those who run in a race allow no hindrances to slow them down, so that they might win a perishable crown; if athletes expose their bodies to the blows of others, driven by the uncertain hope of winning a prize; if merchants venture to the most remote islands of the world for the sake of uncertain profit, undeterred by the most difficult journeys by land and sea, nor by any dangers; if a soldier, motivated by the hope of meager pay, does not hesitate to risk his head and life in the most immediate danger of death; if, finally, the children of this world undertake and endure anything for nearly any ludicrous hope, why should we not even more persistently continue in our race we have begun, casting aside all obstacles, provoked by the certain hope—not of a trivial reward, but truly a blessed hope of heavenly goods? These, with the weight of eternity and immense beatitude, far surpass all the riches of this world by an utterly infinite and incomparable margin (2 Corinthians 4). Therefore, holding onto this hope as an anchor for the soul, both safe and firm, let us persevere in the race with great and lofty spirit, keeping faith and a good conscience, and let us scorn all the trifles of this world, by which Satan seeks to hinder our course and snatch the prize from us, {Hebrews 6} imitating the example of Paul, who commends to his Philippians, writing: "One thing I do: forgetting what is behind and straining toward what is ahead, I press on toward the goal to win the prize for which God has called me heavenward in Christ Jesus" (Philippians 3).

Ninth. The testimony concerning the glorious coming of Jesus Christ for judgment, which is to be noted against the mockers of the last times, who, as Peter foretold, will say: "Where is the promise of His coming? For since the fathers fell asleep, everything continues as it was from the beginning of creation." {2 Peter 3} But we should know that this judgment is decreed by God's unchangeable purpose and promised in His holy Word; therefore, let us remember that it is sinful to doubt it, as mentioned in Isaiah 45, Acts 17, Romans 14, and 2 Corinthians 5.

Tenth. Moreover, the expectation of the coming and appearance of our Lord Jesus Christ should be a most serious exhortation to us for reverence toward the divine majesty and for the pursuit of a life that is holy and pure, since at that time an account will have to be given for everything that we have said or done, whether good or bad, as stated in 2 Corinthians 5, and a sentence of eternal doom, never to be retracted throughout the ages, will be pronounced against all who did not know God and did not obey the Gospel of our Lord Jesus Christ, as noted in 2 Thessalonians 1. Concerning this, Enoch, the seventh preacher of righteousness from the original world [i.e., from creation], already strongly protested against the impious Cainites of his time, as mentioned in the Epistle of Jude. Therefore, let the voice of the eternal Judge always resonate in our ears and minds: "Rise, dead, and come to judgment." Let us always stand as prudent and faithful servants, girded at the loins and awaiting our Master. As mentioned in Luke 12, let us always and unceasingly pray, be sober, and watchful, and not let our hearts be weighed down with gluttony and drunkenness and the cares of this life, so that that day does not suddenly overtake us, for it will come as a thief in the night, like a snare, upon all who dwell on the face of the earth, as Luke 21 warns, so that we are not ashamed at His coming, but having confidence, we may joyfully lift up our heads, for our redemption is drawing near.

Eleventh. We also have a clear testimony of the deity of Christ when Paul, who elsewhere recognizes no other God but the only true God (1 Corinthians 8), nevertheless calls Christ "the great God" without any equivocation, just as elsewhere he proclaims Him to be God blessed forever. And in 1 Timothy 3, discussing His incarnation, he writes that GOD was manifested in the flesh. And in Acts, he asserts that the Church was purchased with the blood of GOD, thereby attributing to Christ the glory and majesty of eternal deity. In this regard, he is in agreement with the unanimous testimony of the Prophets and Apostles, as seen in Isaiah 9 and 35, Jeremiah 23, John 1, and 1 John 5.

Twelfth. Giving Himself for us, Christ displayed His love for us with a testimony more than human, most clearly demonstrated. For as He Himself declares in the Gospel of John: "No one has greater love than this, to lay down one's soul [*animam*] (or life [*vitam*]) for one's friends." But since He laid down His life not for those who by nature would have been friends, but died for enemies, as stated in Romans 5, did He not with that single act open the abyss of His infinite goodness, and pour out and lavish upon us the full force of His astounding love?

Thirteenth. The difference between the death of Christ and that of other men, which is noted in the words of the Apostle, who recounts that Christ gave Himself FOR US—something that cannot be affirmed of other men. Therefore, this death must be not of a mere man, but of God. For as normally it is a man's lot to be born for oneself, not for others; to die for oneself, not for others; so it was for the SON of God to be born FOR US, as stated in Isaiah 9 and Luke 2. It was for the Son of God to die for us, and thus this very one, whom Paul calls the great God, gave HIMSELF for US. Writing to the Galatians, he repeats this, saying: "The life I now live, I live by faith in the Son of God, who (the Son of God) loved me, and gave HIMSELF for me." Hence, the only Son of God was betrayed for us, the Lord of Glory was crucified, and the Author of life was killed, as read in Romans 8, 1 Corinthians 2, and Acts 3. From this, all who wish to be Christians can piously estimate how wondrous and truly ineffable is the κοινωνία [communion] between the Son of God and His Flesh (whose nature was to suffer and die). Because of this, the Flesh of the Savior could not be crucified or delivered to death without the very Son of God, the Author of life, and the Lord of Glory, being truly and actually delivered to death: Not, indeed, according to His divinity, which we know remains eternally unchangeable and immortal, but according to that Flesh, which is not of itself (as it does not subsist by itself) nor of any other than the Son of God, whose Flesh it became, not through a mere union, but one conjoined with the deepest κοινωνία [communion] of the very Natures, without any confusion of them. Without this κοινωνία [communion] of the λόγου [Word] with the Flesh, it would be impossible for the Death of the Humanity to truly pertain to the Son of God in any way—not according to His deity, which we know to be eternally immutable and immortal, but in respect to that Flesh, which is not self-subsistent but truly becomes the proper Flesh of the assuming Son of God: not through a mere union, but a union that is conjoined with the deepest communion of the very Natures, without any confusion between them. Without this communion of the Word with the Flesh, it would be impossible for the Death of the Humanity to truly pertain to the Son of God in any way.

Fourteenth. This reminds us of the atrocity of sin: that to atone for it, no equivalent price could be found other than the Son of God Himself, whose death and blood, as the sole ransom, have redeemed us from iniquity. This consideration should stir in us a hatred for sin, which separates us from God by such a great distance, as Isaiah 59 states. Let us not allow ourselves to be entangled in its deadly snares by the allure of its pleasure; rather, let us remember that beneath its apparent sweetness lies deadly poison, and its bite is more harmful than the strikes of serpents and scorpions, as stated in Sirach 21.

Fifteenth. Furthermore, the doctrine of Justification is explained with its principal causes. The first and supreme one is the grace of God. The second is the merit of Christ. There is also an implicit instrumental cause that apprehends both. Moreover, the final cause is expressed along with the effects of Justification; namely, the salvation of men, the denial of ungodliness, and the zeal for doing good. The Apostle Paul will discuss this topic in detail in the following chapter.

Sixteenth. It is noteworthy what Saint Paul says: That we are redeemed by Christ from ALL iniquity. This shows that Christ did not only make satisfaction for original sin, as if we ourselves are required to make satisfaction for actual sins, as the Scholastic Theologians under the Papacy taught. But Christ has freed us from everything that falls under the name of "ἀνομία" or iniquity, that is, whatever is contrary and hostile to divine Law, through the merit of His obedience and Passion. Hence, John writes: "His blood cleanses us from all sin." {1 John 1 and 2} And He is the propitiation for the sins of the whole world, among which Paul also includes actual sins, no matter how atrocious. For when, in his first letter to the Corinthians, he stated that fornicators, idolaters, adulterers, those who engage in homosexual acts, thieves, the greedy, drunkards, revilers, and robbers will not inherit the Kingdom of God, he immediately adds: "And such were some of you, but you were washed, you were sanctified, you were justified in the name of the Lord Jesus Christ, and by the Spirit of our God." (1 Corinthians 6) Hence, even the thief on the cross did not need any other satisfaction for his horrendous crimes and actual sins than the Passion and death of Christ alone (Luke 23).

Seventeenth. The same is indeed worth noting against the heresy of the Novatians, who denied forgiveness for more serious sins committed after regeneration. However, Paul teaches that no sin should be excluded which does not fall under the infinite merit of Christ and be covered by His blood. But he clearly states that His redemption, without any exception, is effective for atoning for all iniquity, provided that the committed iniquity is deeply lamented and forgiveness for it is sought in Christ.

Eighteenth. This same statement should be directed towards the aim of Scripture, which is consolation. {Rom.15} It often happens that tender consciences are tormented by the sense of their sins, and are so disturbed by the magnitude of these sins that they nearly abandon all hope of obtaining forgiveness for them. Therefore, let such persons be uplifted by these testimonies of the Word of God. It should be emphasized that Christ has liberated not just from some sins, but from all sins universally, provided that the committed iniquity is deeply lamented and its forgiveness is sought in Christ. And thus, against these temptations, let the voice of the Holy Spirit be opposed, which declares that the death of Christ our Savior is so sufficient for the sins of the whole world, that where sin abounded, the grace of God through Jesus Christ our Lord abounded much more. {Rom. 5} And if our sins are like scarlet, yet they shall be purified by the blood of Christ to surpass the whiteness of snow and the purest wool. {Isa. 1}

Nineteenth. The pursuit of new obedience should not be lackluster or cold, but fervent. Therefore, the Christian people are called zealous for good works [ζηλωτην καλῶν ἔργων]. Thus, the feigned obedience of hypocrites, who do all their works not from a burning love of God but to be seen by men, as in Matthew 6 and 23, seeking their own rather than God's glory, does not please God. Nor is the superficial manner of those approved, who mix their good works with sins against conscience, so that if today they do something good, tomorrow they taint that one good deed with many other sins (and these more serious than those that are not consistent with faith). But a fervent zeal and a certain eagerness are required in doing good. This zeal, however, should not be blind, pursuing good works to thereby earn eternal life, but a zeal according to knowledge, directing good works to their true ends: the glory of God and the benefit of one's neighbor. Such was the zeal for good works in those men who are proclaimed perfect and blameless in the Scriptures, not because they provided absolute obedience to God's Law, but because their obedience emanated not from hypocrisy, but from a sincere affection of the heart, as is noted in the Holy Scriptures about Noah, David, Hezekiah, Josiah, Zechariah, and Elizabeth, among other saints.

Twentieth. The duty of teachers primarily lies in speaking or presenting sound doctrine, in urging purity of life, and in rebuking people's errors and sins. Paul admonishes Titus about these aspects of the duty, saying: "Speak these things, and exhort, and rebuke." This role should be directed towards the same goals as the revealed Word of God or the θεόπνευστος (God-breathed) Scripture, which Paul states is useful for teaching, exhorting, and rebuking, as in 2 Timothy 3. Although here we see distinct gifts in ministers, where one may excel in teaching more than in exhorting, another in exhorting and rebuking more than in teaching, each should be equipped in their way and measure with all these, and should not consider themselves fully performing their duty if they only fulfill one of these aspects, neglecting the others. Through teaching, it is necessary to instruct the faith of the listeners; through exhorting, to influence life and morals; through rebuking, it is necessary to criticize those things which either assault doctrine with errors or contaminate the conduct of life. This third aspect, as salt through which people are preserved, must be added, as Christ instructs the Apostles about their duty using this metaphor in Matthew 5 and Mark 9.

Twenty-first. Regarding the obedience to the ministry which Paul demands from the listeners, writing, "Let no man despise you," let the listeners consider that the ministers of the Word are God's envoys, as mentioned in Malachi 2 and 2 Corinthians 5. Those who despise them are despising God, as stated in Luke 10. Just as the Cainites, by scorning Noah, the herald of righteousness, are read to have despised God and contended against His Spirit. More on this topic was discussed in the explanation of the first chapter.

Twenty-second. Since Paul does not want ministers to be despised, he, in turn, requires from them to live in such a way as not to expose themselves to ridicule. Just as among the ministers of the Word, you often find jesters, who with words and deeds prostitute their own authority, which they ought to have in their office. More about this was also said in the first chapter.

Chapter Three.

Argument.

Paul the Apostle continues his discourse, instructing Titus further on what additional duties he should exhort Christians in the Island of Crete to undertake: He assigns a twofold reason, drawn from the circumstances of time, by comparing the previous impious life lived outside Christ in sins, and that life to which they have now arrived through the appearance of God's goodness. He then instructs to avoid useless controversies and to shun heretics who, having been admonished, persist in their heresy. Adding also some private matters, he concludes the Epistle with the customary prayer and wish.

The chapter has four parts: The first is about the admonitions, in addition to the previous ones, that should be given to the Cretans. The second, the reasons with which these admonitions should be fortified. The third, what Titus should avoid in the teaching ministry. The fourth deals with some private matters and greetings.

FIRST PART.

Admonish them) St. Paul wants the Cretans to be admonished chiefly about two things. The first of these is more specific than the other. Initially, he outlines how they ought to behave towards the regular Magistrates or powers. Then, he details the duties by which they should demonstrate their worth to all people indiscriminately.

Regarding the former, Paul thus preaches: **Remind them to be subject to principalities and powers**) "You, my Titus, as a

General Superintendent in Crete, be mindful to urge Christians to obedience towards the Magistrate yourself, and through Ministers under your supervision, take care to diligently remind them: **To be subject to powers and Principalities.** Then they will truly show themselves as subjects, if they obey their edicts and laws." **To be ready for every good work**) He adds a thesis to the hypothesis, and a general principle by a special precept, by which he wants men converted to the faith of the Gospel to be prepared in spirit and duty for every good work, whatever name it goes by. And he illustrates this with the contention of good works opposed to vices: **Not to speak evil of anyone.**) It is a common vice for people to be blind to their own sins but lynx-eyed towards the sins of others, and to seize almost any opportunity to speak ill of their neighbor. This is what Paul wants to be absent from those who profess faith. **Not to be quarrelsome**) This is another vice, from the ugliness of which he wants the conversation of the faithful to be immune, so that they do not fight, either by arguing with words or by fighting with blows. **But humane, etc.**) Just as he generally opposed these vices with the pursuit of good works, so now he elegantly contrasts virtues directly opposed to vices. For the sickness of slander, he opposes ἐπιείκεια or fairness; to the desire to fight, περαότητα or gentleness, the cultivation of which virtues can easily drive out those vices. Therefore he says: **But humane**) In Greek, it is ἐπιεικεῖς. This word signifies fairness, opposed to excessive strictness in judging and criticizing anything. **Showing all gentleness**) As much as piety allows. For sometimes the reason of duty compels us to be severe. Yet this severity in rebuking should be so tinged with gentleness that it is clear we hate the vices of people, not the people themselves. And indeed, he wants this gentleness to be shown towards "all men"—not only towards friends but also towards others, even if they are the most hostile to religion.

Common Places.

First. Here, first of all, those teachers are rebuked who incite the ignorant masses with seditious sermons against the ordinary magistrate, rather than exhorting them to their due obedience. Such were in our time Thomas Müntzer[1], [Henry] Pfeiffer[2], [Nicholas] Storch[3], [Ludwig] Haetzer[4], and other leaders of the Anabaptist faction. They, like torches and trumpets of stubborn rebellion, threw the wretched people into the most disastrous end by calling them away from obedience to the magistrate and inciting them to arms, presenting them to a slaughter that is to be proclaimed for all posterity. Pious ministers should from time to time encourage the people to obey the magistrate, even if he is δυσκόλῳ (difficult) and a tyrant; however, if something is commanded that would not only be unjust in respect to the magistrate who commands it, but also impious in respect to the subjects if they were to carry it out, they should hold to the Savior's Rule: "Render unto Caesar the things that are Caesar's, and unto God the things that are God's" (Matthew 22).

Second. The magistrate is a good ordinance of God, to whose obedience the Apostle subjects Christians. He treats this matter expressly in Romans 13. Therefore, he not only commands obedience to the magistrate but also that public prayers be made for him, as in 1 Timothy 2. Thus, the Anabaptists err in wanting to exclude this

1 Müntzer (1489–1525), violent Anabaptist leader connected with the German Peasant's Revolt of 1525. Müntzer was executed for his actions.
2 Pfeiffer, a former monk, joined Müntzer in the Peasant's Revolt. He, too, was executed after the rebellion.
3 Storch, one of the so-called Zwichau Prophets, an Anabaptist leader of the Abecedarians, who eschewed all education and considered theological study to be idolatry.
4 Haetzer (1500–1529), Anabaptist and likely anti-Trinitarian. Arrested in 1528 in Konstanz on a charge of adultery. Executed in 1529.

state from the boundaries of Christianity, even though it is called by the Apostle's voice the ordinance of God, also confirmed in the New Testament by John the Baptist, Christ, and the Apostles.

Third. We are taught that Christians under the Kingdom of Christ are not bound by the Mosaic forensic laws. For Paul subjects them to the present magistrate, to whom he wants obedience to be rendered. From this, it follows that Christians are also subject to the laws of the present magistrate, for obedience to the magistrate is not rendered unless his laws are obeyed. And it is certainly clear that we are not bound to observe the Mosaic forensic laws, as they are so adapted to the land of Canaan and the character of the Israelite people that it would be absurd to adapt many of them to other places and peoples; for example, those about the division of the land, maintaining the distinction of wealth among the tribes, about marriages, about the return of Israelite property in the Year of Jubilee to its former owners, about the privileges of priests, tithes for the Levites, about choosing a king from only the Israelites, about raising up offspring for a deceased brother from his widow, about polygamy, about divorce, and many others. Therefore, the Lord foretold the abolition of the Israelite policy under the removal of the scepter of Judah (Genesis 49). Meanwhile, we do not deny that there are some Mosaic forensic laws so composed that they can usefully be revived, But not under the assumption that they must be observed because of Moses—whom we know to have been the legislator of the Hebrew people alone—but because they are consistent with the Law of Nature, which binds everyone.

Fourth. Christians should not be prepared for only certain good works, but according to the prescription of the Apostle, for all. "Whatever things are true," he says in Philippians 4, "whatever things are noble, whatever things are just, whatever things are pure, whatever things are lovely, whatever things are of good report, if there is any virtue and if there is anything praiseworthy, meditate on these things." You may find someone who is generous in helping the poor, but suffers from the vice of drunkenness or others, which makes his charity towards the poor futile, while he completely neglects and ignores the virtue of sobriety. "These you ought to have done, without leaving the others undone" (Matthew 23). And "whoever keeps the whole Law and yet stumbles at just one point is guilty of breaking all of it" (James 1). Therefore, let us obey our Apostle, commanding us to be ready for EVERY good work.

Fifth. Concerning the perverse zeal of slandering one's neighbor, which Paul commands us to avoid. For it is contrary to the Commandments of the Decalogue: "You shall not bear false witness." Also: "You shall not kill." But we kill not only with the hand, but often with the tongue, which is sharpened for the destruction of other men, and for this reason is compared to sharp razors and deadly arrows, fire in a thicket, the poison of asps. {Psalms 52, 120, 140} It is called an uncontrollable evil, full of deadly poison, inflicting more bitter wounds on the heart of man than any sword or deadly weapon. {James 3} This formidable scourge is widely described and deplored by the holy men of God, and a huge catalog of evils is listed by Sirach, which are produced by a slanderous and malicious tongue. {Sirach 28} Therefore, let us strive instead to speak well of everyone, even those who persecute us. And following the canon of charity, let us cover the sins of our neighbor, as far as it can be done with a good conscience. This is the laudable ἐπιείκεια (equity) commended to us by the Apostle, which tends to interpret all things in the best part, thinking of removing the beam from one's own eye, rather than from another's (Luke 6).

Sixth. The Apostle repeats a commandment from the sermons of the Savior, given in Matthew 5, which mandates that we should also love our enemies. Thus, our gentleness should not extend only to our friends (for even tax collectors do that, and it would not be remarkable for us to do the same) but also to those who curse us, or as the Apostle here advises, to all people. Such are declared blessed or happy in the very words of Christ Himself: "Blessed are the meek, for they shall inherit the earth." {Matthew 5}

SECOND PART.

Now the Apostle descends to the confirmation of the preceding admonitions, which he fortifies with two very cogent reasons. The first reason is drawn from the circumstance of the preceding time under the former ignorance of Christ. The second is from the time of the manifested divine mercy through the appearance of the Savior Christ.

Thus he writes: **For we ourselves were also once foolish, etc.**) This contains the first reason, in this sense: "We should not be too harsh judges of others' faults. For we too, once, when we still did not know Christ, were prone to various sins." **We were foolish**) He lists a catalog of vices to which they were given before they were enlightened with the knowledge of Christ. He characterizes their condition as foolishness. The Scripture commonly refers to the impious as fools, those deprived of the life-giving recognition of God and Christ, void of the fear of God (which is the beginning of wisdom), ruled by their own passions, understanding only earthly and fleshly things, and without any fear of divine punishment, plunging into all kinds of sins, unaware of the temporal and eternal penalties they are bringing upon themselves. Such folly far surpasses even the most foolish jesters in its stupidity. This vice of spiritual foolishness, as a kind, he now unfolds more deeply in the explanation of its species, as he adds: **Disobedient**) He understands disobedience not only with respect to divine Law, a part of which is known even to those who have not been enlightened by the Gospel of Christ's glory, but also with respect to those who preside over us, whether at home or in public life, such as parents in the family and magistrates in politics. To these, says the Apostle, **we were disobedient**, unruly towards God and men. **Erring**) from the truth of God, from the path of righteousness, from the way of eternal life. Because we did not know Christ, who is the way, the truth, and the life, we were immersed in errors, idolatry, and the deadly darkness of ignorance.

Serving various desires and pleasures) The term **serving** is emphatic, by which Paul notes that intense dedication with which they were wholly carried away and irresistibly drawn to carnal pleasures. They were intensely devoted to these, served them exclusively, and while they wanted to roam freely with unrestrained license, they eagerly bound themselves in the chains of most miserable servitude; namely, to depraved desires. **Living in malice and envy**) **Malice** for the Apostle is the desire to harm one's neighbor; **envy** is the malignant sickness of the soul by which one begrudges the good fortune of others. **Hateful**) στυγητοί ("hateful") means passively. We were most worthy of hatred by God and His angels because of our sins. **Hating one another**) Our hearts were full of hatred and bitterness and in turn, one intensely hated the other. Therefore, he wants to imply: "Since we once were such ourselves, the awareness of our own sins should deter us from that rigor in inquiring too curiously into the lives of others and rather bend us to compassion if we see anyone still subject to that most miserable servitude." **But after that, etc.**) The second reason, which is connected with the former through a clear contrast. He contrasts the unhappiness of the former condition with the incredible blessedness obtained through Christ, in such a way that this part of the contrast also refers to the purpose of persuading Christians to gentleness towards all men, and zeal for doing good. And here, with slightly altered words, he repeats the remarkable commendation of God's goodness proposed at the end of the preceding chapter, to stimulate the pursuit of piety. At the same time, he sets before our eyes the sources and causes of our justification to be considered. **But after the kindness and love of God our Savior toward man appeared, etc.)** The sense is: "I recounted what we once were. However, it is worthwhile to consider what we are now through the rising of divine goodness, and how happily we have struggled from the vast sea of all evils to the harbor of eternal blessedness, so that even the consideration of this fact may inspire us to be grateful towards God and humane towards men." **Appeared**, he says, and like a burst of light from the formidable darkness of earlier times, shone that never enough praised goodness of God, and philanthropy. The Apostle uses two terms to exalt the infallible kindness of God. He calls it σχρησότητα or goodness. Yet God would have remained immutably good even if He had not shown Himself benign to us sinners, but had left us in misery according to the rigor of justice, just as He did with the fallen angels. Now, however, to illustrate His goodness, a certain culmination is added here: that He is not only good in Himself, considered in some immutable goodness, but He also opens the fountain of that goodness to us men, so that He is now σχρησὸς (beneficially good) to us, as He brings forth eternal benefits from the treasures of His goodness. The other term is φιλανθρωπία (philanthropy). As the Latin language cannot render it in one word, so the force of its emphasis cannot be matched by any power of human eloquence. It denotes that amazing love by which the eternal God dignifies mortal man, the Creator dignifies the needy creation, Justice and Holiness dignify miserable sinners, and thus enemies and adversaries, with His heavenly favor, completely wiping out all memory of offenses and establishing a gracious ἀμωησίαν (forgiveness) combined with a perpetual desire to do good.

This is the goodness and φιλανθρωπία (philanthropy) of **our Savior God**, says Paul. Here by the name **Savior**, he does not refer to the second Person of the Trinity, but to the first. For shortly thereafter, he speaks of this Savior God as pouring out the Holy Spirit on us through Jesus Christ. Thus, he distinguishes this Savior from Christ, as Person from Person. For the Father is no less a Savior by virtue of His *mercy* than the Son is by virtue of His *merit*. Moreover, by mentioning the goodness and φιλανθρωπία (philanthropy) of God, he removes all our own merit. Therefore, he adds: **Not by works which are in righteousness, etc.**), as if to say: "This goodness of God is not acquired by our own righteousness, in which we may have performed some external works of the Law; but God preempts all our efforts with His divine benevolence." **According to His mercy, He saved us**, not moved by any worthiness of works performed by us, but rather out of the deep bowels of His Mercy, having pitied our wretched condition, directed His plans toward our salvation, sending His only begotten Son into the world, that He might become a sacrifice for sins.

Through the washing of regeneration, etc.) The instrument of salvation [*instrumentum salutis*], with respect to God offering it, namely Baptism, is expressed. Paul confidently states that God saves us through Baptism, because in Baptism, just as in the Word, God not only offers, but also effectively applies, the salvation obtained through the death of His Son, truly regenerating people, and by the power of His Spirit through this action of Baptism, stimulates faith in them through the power of His Spirit in this act of Baptism. Therefore, he calls it the **washing of regeneration**, in which God, sprinkling with the blood of the Son, cleanses from sins and regenerates the children of wrath to eternal life, thereby renewing and restoring us through His Holy Spirit to the justice and life lost by Adam. For this reason, he also names Baptism as the **washing of the renewal of the Holy Spirit**. In this way, he makes Baptism the instrument (ὄργανον) of salvation due to the associated power of the Holy Spirit. He adds: **Which He poured out on us abundantly, etc.**), where the Holy Spirit, whom he had made the cause of salvation due to the power by which He works life and salvation, he now makes the effect of Baptism, that is, its gifts, which the Lord bestows through Baptism, are shown to be the fruit of Baptism. He amplifies this by showing that it is not with rare drops, but abundantly like a most generous rain, that the Holy Spirit is poured out in Baptism, not only understanding those sanctifying gifts, such as Faith, Regeneration, Charity, etc., but also implying the miraculous gifts commonly used in the early Church, where the Holy Spirit descended upon the baptized, enabling them to speak in new tongues and prophesy. **Through Jesus Christ**) designates the meritorious cause, Jesus Christ, for by the merit of His suffering, He obtained for us the gift of the Holy Spirit. But it also shows the goal of the declared goodness of God, and of the justification that arises from it: **That being justified by His grace, we should become heirs**) By mentioning grace, he again excludes the consideration of works and states this most noble end of Justification: The inheritance of eternal life. Nor does he carelessly add: **according to hope**) for he implies that this inheritance is not laid out before our eyes, nor is it yet actually possessed by the elect, who are known to be subject to the adversities of this world; but it is to be expected in the future, and to be revealed at the coming of Jesus Christ. Lest it seem uncertain because it is not perceptible to the senses, he immediately adds: **This is a trustworthy statement**) teaching that what he discusses about the hope of inheritance is built on much firmer pillars of truth, such that they cannot be moved from the base of their certainty, and that this hope is promised far more sacredly than that it is right to doubt it. **These things I want you to affirm strongly**) He concludes what he said about the goodness of God, and again directs to the goal of his instruction, as if to say: "These are the things, my Titus, that I want you to propose to your listeners, affirm these to them, repeating them frequently, and inculcating them as diligently as possible. So that Christians who have believed, having weighed these reasons in their minds, may strive with all care and concern to diligently labor in the cultivation of good works." However, to add further incentive, he clearly alludes to the sources of honor and usefulness, writing, **these things are honorable** and **profitable to men**, whose beauty and fruits should rightly stimulate a desire for them.

Common Places.

First. It is often necessary to remember our former state, in which we were subject to the tyranny of sin, but not so that we look back at our forsaken lusts with some desire to return to them. For then it would happen to us as Peter warns: "For if, after they have escaped the defilements of the world through the knowledge of the Lord and Savior Jesus Christ, they are again entangled in them and overcome, the last state has become worse for them than the first. For it would have been better for them not to have known the way of righteousness, than having known it, to turn from the holy commandment delivered to them. But it has happened to them according to the true proverb: A dog returns to its own vomit, and a sow, having washed, to her wallowing in the mire." But we must think about our former misery so that we may more deeply recognize the goodness of GOD, who mercifully freed us from it. Then, the memory of our past sins should provide us with an occasion for humility towards God, and equanimity towards our neighbor, lest we condemn others with premature judgment if they have perhaps fallen, as Paul very elegantly advises in Galatians 6. Furthermore, we should henceforth flee from sin all the more diligently, according to the words of Christ: "Behold, you have been made well, do not sin anymore, lest a worse thing come upon you." {John 5.}

Second. The Apostle's admonition provides an example to all ministers of the Word of how exhortations can be usefully formed; namely, for the sake of mitigation, they should sometimes use the figure of communication, or κοινωποιήσεως [communion or participation], and including themselves in the exhortation, just as Paul does when he does not speak only of the Cretans and what they once were, but also including himself, he says: "We ourselves were also once foolish, etc." In this way, the listener understands that such admonitions or corrections do not emanate from a heart bursting with emotions, but from a sincere desire for the conversion and salvation of men.

Third. The saints should be so disposed that they do not hide their sins, but willingly confess them publicly, if necessary. The Apostle does this when he includes himself among others in the list of those who were once foolish and disobedient, and contaminated with other sins. Similarly, Isaiah, on behalf of himself and the people, says: "We are all as an unclean thing, and all our righteousnesses are as filthy rags" (Isaiah 64). And Daniel recognizes not only the sins of the people, but also his own [sins] through a frank confession: "We have sinned, and have committed iniquity, etc." (chapter 9). Let us do the same: Not try to defend our errors, but rather willingly confess them with a hand upon our mouth. {Job 39} "If we confess our sins, He is faithful and just to forgive us our sins, and to cleanse us from all unrighteousness" (1 John 1).

Fourth. By these very examples of the Prophets and Apostles who did not even in their writings hide the sins to which they were subject, we are clearly instructed about the truth and certainty of the Prophetic and Apostolic Scripture. This is admirably defended from any suspicion of fraud because they themselves preferred to reveal their own sins to the whole world rather than detract from the integrity of the Biblical narrative. Thus, Moses reveals his disbelief at the waters of Meribah. Similarly, Paul in this place counts himself among those who were once foolish, etc., and elsewhere admits that he was a persecutor, a blasphemer, and a violent destroyer of churches. So Matthew does not hesitate to confess that he was among those who, because of their tax collecting, were utterly infamous (chapter 9). This is something that other, profane writers do not do, who in any case either completely conceal their crimes or paint and disguise them with contrived colors.

Fifth. It is notable that the Holy Spirit's judgment of the wicked is that they are foolish. Just as the world considers the pious to be foolish (as in Wisdom 2 and 5, Acts 26), and regards all their wisdom as folly: so, in turn, the Holy Spirit deems the impious to be foolish. And rightly so. For if those are considered foolish in human affairs who are devoid of understanding of human matters, how much more foolish are those who are lacking in the knowledge of divine matters, in which salvation rests? If we regard as foolish and insane those who harm themselves, who inflict violence upon themselves—how much more insane are those who willingly rush into eternal damnation? If you would consider foolish someone who would trade a noble horse for a flute, how much more foolish is he who exchanges eternal goods for temporal ones, and for the pleasure or gain of a brief moment, makes himself an outcast from the kingdom of heaven? Therefore, let us not be children in understanding, but in malice be children. Let us walk circumspectly, not as unwise, but as wise. The beginning and foundation of this wisdom is the fear of the Lord. This fear makes the foolish wise, as Scripture frequently says.

Sixth. Concerning disobedience, which is a certain fruit of the previously mentioned foolishness or impiety. Indeed, he who is truly wise fears God, and he who fears God honors the King, as Peter says: honors parents, respects the ministers of the divine Word, and exhibits to them the obedience prescribed by the word of the Lord. {1 Peter 2}

Seventh. Regarding the natural misery of all men, which Paul expresses by calling those who are alien to the knowledge of Christ 'wanderers.' And such were all of us once. We all had turned away from the path of piety and were like wandering sheep. Each one followed their own way. {Isaiah 53, 1 Peter 2} But thanks be to God, for we have turned to the Bishop of our souls, who came to seek and save what was lost (Matthew 18). However, when we are called away from the path of unrighteousness, let us not be of a mind to want to persevere in error. This is what Jeremiah laments about the Jews, and this had been their undoing. {Jeremiah 8}

Eighth. Regarding the sad and ignoble servitude to which men are subjected when they serve carnal desires. Such men, when they seem to themselves most free, doing whatever pleases the flesh, are in fact most enslaved. As it is written: "He who commits sin is a slave to sin." {John 8} It is well known what the wages of this unhappy lord are, which he pays to his servants and worshippers; namely, confusion and eternal death (Romans 6). "For if you live according to the flesh, you will die," says the Apostle in Romans 8. Peter describes their misery, joined with the vain persuasion of freedom, while discussing the false teachers in this way: They entice men through the lusts of the flesh, through much wantonness, those who were truly escaping from those who live in error, while they promise them freedom, though they themselves are the slaves of corruption. For by whom a man is overcome, to that he is enslaved (2 Peter 2). On the contrary, the yoke of Christ, under which we have become servants of righteousness, is the highest and most noble freedom, yielding the fruit of sanctification and, in the end, eternal life. {Matthew 11} For the wages of sin is death. But the gift of God is eternal life through Jesus Christ our Lord. {Romans 6}

Ninth. Concerning avoiding malice and envy, as such vices are diametrically opposed to Christian love: Charity does not harm the enemy, but rather, as Christ and Paul testify and advise, does good to him. {Matthew 5, Romans 12} Charity does not envy, charity does not think evil (1 Corinthians 13). Therefore, by cherishing charity with the utmost devotion, we will easily restrain ourselves from such malice and envy.

Tenth. Concerning the infinite goodness and mercy of the Lord, in that He showed Himself so merciful to us, miserable and unworthy sinners, that He did not wish us to be condemned (as, for example, the fallen angels), but eternally saved. Moved by His goodness, He sent His only begotten Son as a propitiation for the world, as John writes in 1 John 4. This is such a sublime benefit that the angels of heaven long to look into it, and the Apostle Paul earnestly triumphs from it, saying: "What, then, shall we say to these things? If God is for us, who can be against us? He who did not spare His own Son, but gave Him up for us all, how will He not also, along with Him, graciously give us all things?" etc. {Romans 8}

Eleventh. Concerning the Justification of the sinful man before God, which Paul describes in such a way as to make it clear that it is done solely by the mercy of God through Jesus Christ, without our works. Therefore, those who assert and declare that God takes into account our works in the Justification of the sinful man deviate from Paul's teaching. And it is noteworthy that by this Pauline canon, not only are the works of unregenerated men excluded, but generally all our works, which we do ourselves. Indeed, the regenerated do perform their own works and are in a certain way (although with granted strength) co-workers (σύνεργοι) with the

Holy Spirit in producing them. Therefore, these, too, are excluded from the realm of Justification. This is why even the regenerated Abraham was not justified by any works, as Moses most clearly teaches, and which Paul explains more fully in the New Testament. Therefore, let us not attribute our Justification, even as the regenerate, to any works, under whatever name they may come, except the single work of Christ's obedience. For it is not our new obedience that justifies, but as it is written: "Just as through the disobedience of one man the many were made sinners, so also through the obedience of the ONE, the many will be made righteous." {Romans 5} Therefore, Paul clearly denies the justifying power of his new obedience and its works: "I am not aware of anything against myself, but I am not thereby acquitted" (1 Corinthians 4). What we say also becomes clear from this: Because St. Paul not only removes all works at once from establishing Justification (since he asserts we are justified by His grace: "But if it is by grace, it is no longer on the basis of works," Romans 11), but he also removes works from salvation, saying not only that we are justified by the grace of God, but also that He saved us by His mercy, without the works that we do. This is confirmed in Romans 4, where he notes that David defines OUR BLESSING as the imputation of righteousness without works. And in Ephesians 2, he says: "By grace you have been SAVED through faith, and this is not from yourselves. It is the gift of God, not a result of works, so that no one may boast." Therefore, the fabrication falls apart, by which the imposters and soul thieves, the Jesuits, deceive many by mixing the works of the reborn into the matter of achieving salvation: Whose opinion, if it were true, certainly if not Justification, then Salvation or beatification [*Saluatio vel beatificatio*] would be assigned to works, contrary to the clear assertion of our Apostle.

Twelfth. It is most diligently to be noted here: Although Justification and Salvation are placed by the Apostle solely in the mercy of God, by no means does this loosen the reins to the license of sinning; instead, it most effectively stimulates towards piety. For Paul derives an argument from this to persuade people to the practice of piety, and thus he asserts that we are saved without works, but he wants this very doctrine of Justification without works to be presented to people also with this intention: That they should excel in good works, and this follows with the best of consequences. For the greater the benefit of God saving us out of mere mercy, the more fervent gratitude is required, the greater the effort to obey such a Benefactor. This is what we see in Zacharias, the father of John the Baptist, understanding when he sings that God, out of His mercy promised to our fathers, has delivered us from the hand of our enemies. But what then? To sin more freely afterwards? Not at all. But he says, "to serve Him in holiness and righteousness before Him all the days of our life," as this place [*locus*] was treated in the preceding chapter and confirmed by the testimonies of the Holy Scriptures.

Thirteenth. This notable Apostolic text also teaches us about Baptism: that it is not merely some sign of regeneration, as the impious theologians of today, colluding with the Schwenckfeldians, teach. These theologians, due to an absolute decree of predestination born in their own brains, almost completely empty the entire ministry of its power, and here, too, they forge metonymies. But we, with the Apostle, establish that Baptism is the washing of regeneration, by which we are so truly cleansed from sins that Paul does not hesitate to affirm that God saves us through this washing of regeneration. For Christ cleanses His Church with the washing of water through the Word (Ephesians 5), Christ Himself attesting and saying: "Unless one is born of water and the Spirit, he cannot enter the kingdom of heaven." For it seemed good to God to work regeneration and faith, by which eternal salvation is grasped, through the Baptism of water as though by an instrument, by the power of His Spirit. Therefore, when fanatics object: "There is only one organic cause of salvation, Faith. Therefore, Baptism is not an instrument of regeneration and salvation," here the objection is dissolved by distinction: Indeed, there is only one instrument GRASPING salvation, namely faith, besides which there is no other grasping organ. But then there are instruments OFFERING salvation, with respect to God, by which God offers Salvation and His Grace, and at the same time works and excites in us that private instrument; namely, faith. Thus, through Baptism, God offers His grace, and at the same time stimulates [excitat] in us the grasping instrument (that is, faith), because He stimulates regeneration through Baptism, with which (regeneration) faith is always and perpetually connected in an indivisible association. Just as also through the Gospel, God both offers grace and works faith and salvation, as Paul says: "The Gospel is the power of God for salvation to everyone who believes." {Romans 1 and 10} And again: "Faith comes from hearing."

Fourteenth. Note here also the treachery of the Anabaptists, who deprive and dispossess infants of such a necessary instrument of salvation. Who needs washing, if not the unclean? Are not even infants unclean? For who can bring a clean thing out of an unclean? {Job 14} Therefore, infants need to be washed from the sins in which they were conceived and born (Psalm 51). Hence, Christ confirms to Nicodemus: "Unless one is born of WATER and the Spirit, he cannot enter the kingdom of heaven." And lest anyone think this applies only to adults, He adds: "That which is born of the flesh is flesh"; that is, it is polluted before God and liable to condemnation. Who does not know that this birth from the flesh occurs in infancy itself? Therefore, it is necessarily concluded from here that infants, too, must be baptized.

Fifteenth. Concerning the gift of the Holy Spirit, which is the fruit of our Baptism, for there we are anointed, endowed, and sealed with the Holy Spirit. Although He does not work in us those miraculous gifts that were customary in the time of the early Church, He still works more necessary gifts: Faith, regeneration, sanctification, etc. Therefore, let us be careful not to grieve the Holy Spirit of God, by whom we have been sealed for the day of redemption (Ephesians 4).

Sixteenth. The word "renovation" reminds us of the newness of life, that by mortifying sin and crucifying the old man with his desires, we should henceforth serve God in the newness of life, as those who, having been renewed in the spirit of our minds, have put on the new man, who is created according to God, in righteousness and the holiness of truth. {Romans 6, Galatians 5, Ephesians 4}

Seventeenth. A testimony concerning the Trinity, whose Persons are all expressed here, where it is said that God the Father pours out the Holy Spirit through Jesus Christ. And indeed, that the Father is God is seen from the work assigned to Him (to say nothing of infinite other things), because He pours out and sends the Holy Spirit, which is a work of divine Majesty. That Jesus Christ is God is apparent (just as I pass over countless other arguments and criteria) from the fact that the Holy Spirit is poured out through Him, that is, through His infinite merit. This likewise demonstrates His eternal Deity. Thirdly, because the work of renewal and the power suitable only to God, and consequently the glory of Deity, is attributed to the Holy Spirit.

Eighteenth. It is also noteworthy that all three Persons work together in accomplishing our salvation. God the Father is the One who saves us by His mercy alone, and He sends the Son for this purpose. The Son, coming into the world, obtains for us this mercy of the Father: He obtains salvation, He obtains the gift of the Holy Spirit. The Holy Spirit is the One who, by His power in Baptism, regenerates us to eternal life, effectively arousing faith in us. He also renews us so that, having put to death the old Adam, we may henceforth walk in newness of life and not fall again from the grace of God. This matter demonstrates that the entire Trinity labors in the completion of our salvation and that our God is truly the God who saves men, and therefore the God who proclaims in Isaiah 43, "I am Jehovah, and besides Me there is no Savior."

Nineteenth. Concerning the inheritance of eternal life, to which we should rightly aspire, and take care not to lose. For if no one is so foolish as to wish to renounce an earthly inheritance, how much more effort should be made not to be deprived of the heavenly inheritance? This happens to all those who intentionally sin against God's Law and will. As it is written: "Neither fornicators, nor idolaters, nor adulterers, nor effeminate, etc., will inherit the kingdom of God" (1 Corinthians 6).

Twentieth. Concerning the Christian hope, by which we await the good things hidden in Christ and to be revealed to the children of God, namely the inheritance of an incorruptible life. Concerning this Christian virtue, it is written in Romans 8, "For in this hope we were saved. Now hope that is seen is not hope. For who hopes for what he sees? But if we hope for what we do not see, we wait for it with patience." Paul testifies that this hope is certain. After having said that we are heirs according to the hope of eternal life, he adds that the word is indisputable. Indeed, as he writes in Romans 5, "Hope does not put us to shame."

Twenty-first. Since Paul repeatedly says: "Speak these things; I want you to affirm these things, etc.," Pastors of the Church are reminded not to tire of constantly inculcating to their listeners the doctrine of Justification and the pursuit of good works, nor should they be eager to devise something new to capture the fancy of the crowd. As is often found, some think it unseemly to repeat the same thing over and over, and consider it much more glorious to present something new and previously unheard. However, it is better to remember this admonition of Paul, which he himself illustrates by example in Philippians 3: "To write the same things to you is not irksome for me, and it is safe for you." How necessary it is to constantly reiterate the necessary doctrine due to the great ignorance of the common people is too well taught by daily experience.

Twenty-second. Concerning pursuing not those things that please the flesh or appear useful according to the world, but those that are truly honorable and useful: Those things are truly honorable which God commands and which are in accord with His holy will; dishonorable are those that are in disagreement [with God's command and will]. Those are truly useful which bring not transitory, but eternal goods, such as piety, which is great gain and useful for everything, having promises not only for this life but also for the future. {1 Timothy 4 and 6} For by His grace, the Lord will adorn the labors of His faithful with greater glory in eternal life, giving to each one according to his labor, as Paul asserts (1 Corinthians 3).

THIRD PART.

So far, St. Paul has carefully explained what he wants Titus to do in his teaching role. Now he warns him what to avoid in this arduous office. First, Paul says: **But avoid foolish questions, etc.**) He calls **foolish** those curious and useless questions that contain no divine wisdom and from which no benefit accrues to the Church.

He also instructs to avoid **genealogies**, to which the Jews at that time were excessively devoted. Although these once had their use in the Old Testament, and were very important for maintaining the distinction of tribes, which the Lord wanted to be separate until the coming of Christ so that it might be more certain from which tribe He was to come, after Christ's arrival and revelation to the Hebrew nation, the Levitical Priesthood was abolished, for which genealogies were likewise to be observed (as it is read in Nehemiah that some, having lost their genealogy, were commanded to abstain from the priesthood until a priest arose with Urim and Thummim). After also making one people out of two, Jewish and Gentile, by demolishing the dividing wall through Christ, namely the law in decrees of ceremonies, there was no further use for genealogies. Moreover, they had fallen into such disuse that they could no longer be precisely known due to several dispersions of the people. Nonetheless, as if almost the entire religion consisted in these, the Jews were devoted to them to the point of superstition, spending much time and labor investigating them without any fruit or benefit. Therefore, he wants these to be avoided, as they are a waste of oil and effort in their investigation. **Contentions** or **legal disputes** he calls those which the Jews raised about the observance of circumcision, the distinction of foods, Jewish ceremonies, etc.

He similarly wants these to be foreign to Titus, adding the reason of being useless: **For they are**, he says, **useless**, because they offer no edification. They are **superfluous**, which can and should be cut off, and only useful things are to be taught and learned, by which either a man's faith may be instructed in the knowledge of the necessary Heads of celestial doctrine [*Capitum doctrinae coelestis*], or minds may be formed in the practice of piety. **A man that is a heretic, etc.**) The second thing he instructs to avoid is the **heretic**, who either invents false doctrines anew or obstinately defends those devised by others. He shows what process should be undertaken with such a person. He wants him first to be **admonished** and convinced, by showing the error from the Holy Scriptures. And this should be done once and then again. But if he does not come to his senses, but defends his preconceived opinion with stubborn zeal, he instructs further that such a person should be **avoided**, giving this reason: that in recalling him, every stone is moved in vain. **Knowing that he that is such is subverted**, so as not to return. **And sins, being condemned by himself** (ἀυτοκατάκριτους), who, convinced in his own conscience of the error, nevertheless knowingly and willingly defends it with obstinate malice, and entices others into his snare by arguing.

Common Places.

First. What Paul proposes to Titus about avoiding useless questions, let all Pastors consider it spoken to themselves. Let them not weary themselves with thorny questions, nor delight in raising them for the sake of capturing vain glory, whether in the public assembly of the Church or in private conversations. They should consider how such questions entangle the minds of men with snares of doubt, which the devil seizes to either throw the simple into perverse opinions or serious temptations, or to make them profane, so that they exercise their wit in sacred matters and, like the Skeptics, call everything into doubt through argument. By this means, piety towards God and His Word is extinguished, and the hearts of men are entangled with infinite doubts, so that shipwreck of faith is most to be feared in this regard. Pious teachers should imitate the manner of God, who says in Isaiah 48: "I am the Lord your God, who teaches you what is beneficial."

Second. From this, it can also be seen what should be thought of the most thorny disputes of the Sophists of the Papal Kingdom.

For the Scholastic Doctors, the Seraphic Thomas[5], Subtle Scotus[6], *Dormi secure*[7], Alexander of Hales[8], [Robert] Holcot[9], and other monstrosities of vain theologians, what did they largely deal with other than the most idle questions, in which not even a morsel of theological learning or religious piety was present? Hence, fables about Purgatory; hence, disputes about the Choirs of Angels and Celestial Hierarchies. Hence, questions about what a mouse gnaws if it eats consecrated bread, and countless others. We are indeed glad to be freed from these, and should be grateful to God that with the rise of the Gospel, the murky pools of the Sophists have been blocked, and the crystal-clear springs of the Holy Scriptures have been opened to us, and the opportunity given to draw from there what contributes to everlasting salvation.

Third. Regarding Genealogies, which are not universally condemned. Indeed, they have their use, especially in illustrious families. However, princes and magnates should engage in their consideration in such a way that they do not become arrogant due to the fame of their lineage, or look down upon those of lower status. For whatever is exalted among men is an abomination in the sight of God. Since He is not a respecter of persons, and in His sight, we are all of the same origin and condition, conceived and born in sins, therefore, as a most serious enemy and hater of all pride, He has cast down and submerged the most illustrious families from

---

5 Thomas Aquinas (1225–1274), Dominican. Today, the most well-remembered of the Scholastics.

6 Duns Scotus (1263–1308), Franciscan.

7 The reference is to a collection of 71 sermons by Johannes de Verdena (d. 1437), *Sermones 'Dormi secure' de tempore*. It was considered a collection of sermons for clergy to lazy to compose their own.

8 Alexander of Hales (1185–1245), Franciscan. He received the appellation, *Doctor Irrefragibilis* (Irrefutable Teacher).

9 Robter Holcot (1290–1349), Dominican. He was known as *Doctor firmus et indefatigabilis* (Strong and Tireless Teacher).

their heights of dignity into the mire of oblivion, and erased them like mud in the streets; conversely, He has raised the poor from the dungheap and set them among princes. Instead, they [i.e., princes and magnates] should strive for true nobility, which is conferred by the love of heavenly wisdom, for this bestows an immortal name upon its followers, so that their memory may be in eternal blessing, and their names no longer counted in human genealogy, but written in heaven (Luke 10, Philippians 4).

Fourth. The admonition to avoid a heretic clearly teaches that there have always been, and will continue to be, heretics, who are either the authors of new dogmas or their defenders. Thus, there has never been a century so blessed that it did not have such individuals. This is clearly taught by Paul in 1 Corinthians 11, where he says, "For there must be heresies among you." For Satan often stirs up clever minds, using them as sharp tools to deceive people. Therefore, those who complain about being born in this era, where the Christian world is shaken by so many dissensions, are unjust critics. But this is not new, as is evident both from this testimony of Paul and from other instances that occur everywhere.

Fifth. We are also warned concerning the process by which we should deal with heretics. Indeed, that they should not be tolerated or given the chair [*cathedram*] of the Church is self-evident. The Catholics believe that they should be removed from human affairs by sword, flame, noose, and other punishments, and under this pretext, they—the mother of harlots and abominations of the earth, Roman Babylon, eagerly kindling the Babylonian furnace, and long drunk with the blood of the saints, and with the blood of the martyrs of Jesus—rage against the true servants and confessors of Jesus Christ. But this is by no means the legitimate way to proceed. For it has never pleased anyone good to rage unto death even against a convicted heretic. {Augustine} But this is the Apostolic process: That heretics should be convinced by the Word of God, that the falsehood of errors be uncovered, and the truth be demonstrated—and this not only once, but after one or two admonitions. However, if they continue to be obstinate, they should be avoided as cut off from the communion of the Church, according to Christ's command: "Beware of false prophets." Also: "Leave them; they are blind guides." And pious magistrates will consider by what means it can be prevented that they insinuate themselves stealthily among the ignorant common people as they seek to sow and overturn them with their heresy.

Sixth. Paul's admonition about heretics provides a definition of the sin against the Holy Spirit. For this sin is not committed in life and morals, but in doctrine: When one acknowledges the truth of the doctrine, and not only deviates from the recognized doctrine, but also, αὐτοκατάκριτους (self-condemned), attacks it. This is what the Pharisees do when, convinced in their hearts by the evident signs of Jesus, nevertheless attribute them to Beelzebub, the prince of demons, against the testimony of their own conscience. There are many such among heretics, who are convicted of error but do not repent of it, lest they seem to have erred, but rather knowingly oppose and prefer to blaspheme heavenly truth than to recognize and confess their error. Although we should not easily or hastily judge anyone as being guilty of this enormous sin, the Apostle here writes not without reason: "KNOW that such a one is subverted, and sins αὐτοκατάκριτους (self-condemned)." For when solid admonition has preceded once or twice, by which he is so convinced that he can bring forth nothing even having the appearance of truth, it is evident, from this and other indications and circumstances, that he truly is convicted and opposes his own conscience when he fights against the demonstrated truth. And indeed, they do not return, but are subverted, says the Apostle, having been given over to the full power of the devil, who hardens them so that they no longer even wish to return or be saved. Hence it happens that because of the very certain hardening attached to them, their sin becomes unforgivable, as Christ says. Not that it could not be forgiven even by the infinite merit of Christ if they aspired to grace, but because they do not even desire grace, perpetually defending falsehood against their conscience in a sort of stupor, and opposing the acknowledged truth. However, if such people, who had truly previously sinned against the Holy Spirit, were to return or earnestly aspire to grace, there is no doubt that they would be saved through the merit of Christ, which is a sufficient ransom (λύτρον) for the sins of the whole world, and thus also for this sin of blasphemy against the Holy Spirit. This is so true that, even though the Lord had gravely accused the Pharisees of this serious sin, He nevertheless adds: "Either make the tree good and its fruit good, or make the tree bad and its fruit bad," clearly teaching that even after committing that sin, if they had turned to the Shepherd of souls ,Jesus Christ, they would undoubtedly have been received, and the bad tree would have been changed into a good one. {Matthew 12} But as I said, this condition is not fulfilled by them: Indeed, they do not even wish it, because of the extreme and final hardening attached to them, which, having been delivered to seven evil spirits, are most strongly occupied by them, so that they no longer turn back and are healed.

FOURTH PART.

This final part contains some personal matters. For he asks that Titus come to **Nicopolis**, a city in Macedonia (where the Apostle was then staying and had **decided to spend the winter**) if he summons him either through **Artemas** or **Tychicus** (who is also mentioned in Acts 20, Ephesians 6, Colossians 4, 2 Timothy 4). The reason for desiring his coming was none other than to confer with him face-to-face about the state of the Cretan churches, to correct anything that required it, with prompt counsel and remedy. **Bring Zenas the lawyer and Apollo, etc.**) He asks Titus to send from the island of Crete **Zenas** (who appears to have converted from Judaism to the faith of Christ, as he is called a **lawyer**, that is, well-versed in the law of Moses). Then **Apollos**, the man fervent in the zeal of the truth of the Gospel doctrine. His commendable praise is evident in Acts 18, as well as in the first letter to the Corinthians 1, 3, and 4. He wants these two to be sent ahead for certain reasons, which he does not express here. In general, we know that Paul sought nothing other in such delegations than to share his plans for planting churches with pious teachers and to hear their judgments in turn. Therefore, he asks for these two to be sent and **carefully provided for, so that they lack nothing** for their journey. **And let our people also learn to maintain good works**) He shifts from the hypothesis to the thesis, and what he had said about Titus, to see that nothing was lacking for those he was about to send ahead, now applies to the rest, whether Cretans or other Christians, that they **maintain good works**, aiding with their resources and expenses the progress of the Gospel, and all things that pertain to the promotion of Gospel teaching.

Greetings, etc.) He greets Titus in the name of those Christians who were with Paul in Nicopolis, and he himself greets those in the island of Crete who **love him**, and the other fellow workers of the Word of God **in faith**. Having thus settled all these matters, he concludes the letter with a prayer or wish, with which he had also begun it: **The grace of God be with all of you, AMEN.**

Common Places.

First. Concerning the sharing of counsel in matters pertaining to faith and the confession of doctrine, which is very beneficial and useful. Therefore, timely counsel is introduced, and Pastors should hold meetings [*conuentus*] to deliberate on matters that contribute to building up the Church and averting offenses. The Lord wishes to be present at these meetings according to His promise (Matthew 18).

Second. That this notable Apostle willingly hears the advice, wishes, and judgments of others, and does not undertake everything alone without consulting others, teaches Church Doctors, however adorned with sublime gifts, not to look down upon others as inferiors. Jethro, Moses' father-in-law, though unequal in the measure of gifts to his son-in-law, was able to suggest beneficial advice by which the burden of his labors could be alleviated. Inferiors can still give counsel to those more learned, which they themselves had not considered. Paul certainly does not doubt that he could gain the fruit of mutual consolation from the conduct of the Romans— he who was divinely taught in God's own Paradise in a singular way and illuminated with the deepest knowledge of theological matters. Why, then, should we be ashamed to listen to the opinions of others? Especially when God often suggests to those of lower order what escapes the higher or about which they themselves think less.

Third. Concerning the pursuit of good works, about which it has been spoken several times in the explanation of the Epistle.

Fourth. Specifically, Christians are admonished that, when necessary, they should support their religion even with their own expenses, and generously help those who labor in promoting the course of heavenly doctrine. In the past, people used to contribute generously to promote idolatry, and deprive their own household, just to fatten Epicurean swine, lazy and slothful bellies: Monks and impure priests. The expenses bestowed upon them perished just as if one had thrown them into a flowing river. Why, then, are people so stingy and reluctant in promoting the course of the Gospel?

True Christians should remember Paul's command in Galatians 6: "Let the one who is taught the word share all good things with the one who teaches." Remember also the promise added there: "And let us not grow weary of doing good, for in due season we will reap, if we do not give up."

Fifth. Concerning the greetings of Christians, which are pregnant with the blessing of God, if they are received in faith. For thus Christ says in Matthew 10, "If you enter a house, greet it, and if the house is worthy, let your peace come upon it." Therefore, the mutual greeting of the faithful is not just a civil custom, but a pious wish, by which they pray for each other's good from God. Therefore, if the Gentiles have given this command to their people—to greet each other with a certain love of civility—how much more rightly should Christians greet each other, whose greetings carry with them the blessing of God? For this reason, in his Epistles, Paul frequently reminds Christians to greet each other with a holy kiss.

SOLI DEO GLORIA.

www.ingramcontent.com/pod-product-compliance
Lightning Source LLC
Chambersburg PA
CBHW060053100426

42742CB00014B/2807